Serenity
DAWNS

Serenity DAWNS

W. 'Speedy' Moore

AMBASSADOR

Belfast Northern Ireland **Greenville** South Carolina

ISBN 1 84030 089 2

Ambassador Publications
a division of
Ambassador Productions Ltd.
Providence House
Ardenlee Street,
Belfast,
BT6 8QJ
Northern Ireland
www.ambassador-productions.com

Emerald House
427 Wade Hampton Blvd.
Greenville
SC 29609, USA
www.emeraldhouse.com

Preface

LIKE ALL FINE JOURNALISTS WILLIAM 'SPEEDY' MOORE
IS BLESSED WITH A GIFT. HE IS A GREAT STORYTELLER.

Throughout his long remarkable career as a newspaper
columnist, broadcaster and author, Speedy has displayed an uncanny
ability to connect with his legions of fans in Ireland and overseas.
People love his stories because they are the stories of their lives and
the stories of the lives of their families and ancestors. They are the
stories of Irish folk with their unique culture, their interesting
history and their distinctive sense of humour.

This new book reaffirms Speedy's reputation as one of our
favourite storytellers. In many ways it is the story of his life ... a life
enriched by a wonderful family and an incredible assortment of
friends; a life full of trials and tribulations; a life culminating in
amazing success and personal rewards in spite of his constant battle
against his own personal demons.

When we read Speedy's stories we marvel once again at his skills
in communicating with "his" audience and we marvel at his

resilience. We also experience the joy of another captivating, sometimes hilarious journey into the Ulster countryside and the warm-hearted people who have made it such a special place.

Bob Culbert
Commissioner of Documentaries for CTV Television Network, Canada.
Former Executive Director of Network TV News, Current Affairs and Newsworld All News Channel, Canadian Broadcasting Corporation.

Foreword

IT HAS BEEN MY PRIVILEGE TO READ THE MANUSCRIPT OF 'SPEEDY' MOORE'S AUTOBIOGRAPHY AND I thoroughly enjoyed its every line and phrase, written in that unique style which has captivated readers for more than a record seven decades and is still doing so.

I reckon the passing of the years has hardened my outlook on living, yet I confess to finding the deeper emotions stirred as the 88 year old author reflects on his boyhood and youth when the poor endured unspeakable hardships and a place in the degrading depths destitution creates - a humiliating and sordid history of just two generations ago.

I laughed heartily at his reams of Irish wit. Gleaned from all types of characters, here, there and everywhere and from turf fire gatherings in mountains and valleys those humorous anecdotes, described in his inimitable trend, are really outstanding. And the old sayings he quotes are not without considerable logic.

Speedy getting caught in the web of strong drink and becoming a mental and physical wreck before serenity dawns in his broken and tortured life are particularly moving and gripping chapters, which provide definite proof that there is an escape route from the curse, thus illuminating a ray of hope for its countless victims.

For his admirable contribution to Northern Ireland journalism over the long years Speedy received the M.B.E. in 1995 - an honour which earned the acclaim of his press colleagues, and he has many.

This new publication will suit all literary tastes and be read over and over again for the immense interest its pages evoke.

John Watt
Broadcaster and journalist

List of CONTENTS

Dedication

**To my wife
Margaret.**

Chapter
ONE

NOVEMBER 30th,1912, WAS THE DAY I WAS DELIVERED TO THE LOVELY MARY EDITH MOORE, AT HER HOME IN Abbey Street, Coleraine, Northern Ireland, and family records reveal little happenings that took place just before my birth and directly after it.

When I was well on the way, Mary Edith's schoolgirl daughters, Etta, Jeannie and Annie, kept putting awkward questions to her about her abnormal size and the gentle woman could only ward them off with feeble answers, for in that far-off era, parents never discussed pregnancy with children. They were made to believe that little brothers and sisters were brought by a stork, a huge bird which held each bundle of joy securely in its long beak.

Therefore, on Mary Edith entering labour and the midwife, Nurse Lucas, being called, the inquisitive daughters, on finishing at school that memorable day, were ordered to stay with an aunt, who lived a short distance from Abbey Street.

Thankfully everything was to the midwife's satisfaction and I was born at 4pm, lively and healthy and weighing 9lb.

When my father came home from work a couple of hours later he slipped upstairs to the scene of birth, looked down on me shyly as he twisted his cap with shaking hands. Then, not having uttered a word, he turned and ran to where my sisters were and shouted: "Mister Stork has brought you the gift of a wee brother!"

They, bless them, cheered and danced and sang and then begged father to take them home immediately to see their wee new brother. Christmas had come early for them.

Soon news of my birth was circulating over a network of tongues with incredible speed until everyone in Abbey Street and adjacent streets knew.

Such interest and means of communication were not derived through the Moore family holding any special position in local society. Eighty eight years ago when radio and television were unknown and morning newspapers sparse, all births and weddings within the working-class community proved to be welcome items for discussion.

At 7.30pm on the evening of my birth, relatives and friends of the family came to congratulate my mother and father and participate in the traditional pass-around ritual, which meant me being lifted from the warmth and comfort of mother's side and handed to each person in the room, who gave me a cuddle before making their comment, some of which were: "A big bonnie bouncin' wane." "As healthy as a trout." "Has an intelligent brow." "You certainly can't deny that one Willie. It's as like you as are two peas in a pod."

James Parkhill, my mother's brother, was the last of the well-wishers to handle me. And he showed his appreciation of my arrival by giving me a couple of powerful shoulder-high swings to left and right, before waltzing me over to the bed and laying me back at the side of my mother, who gave a deep sigh of relief.

I was named William for my father, so to save confusion when discussing us I was referred to as Wee Willie and he as Big Willie.

The title suited father, for he was a huge man towering to 6ft 3ins with build in neat proportion. He had to be big and strong for the job he did as a haulier for the Railway Company.

His wages were fourteen shillings for a 62 hour week and the one affectionate thing that can be written about his life of abject slavery was his mare Molly. Almost human she would not pass our house until my mother or some other member of the family stroked her silken mane and treated her to a griddle-baked soda scone.

Indeed, when I started taking my first uncertain steps the thrill of giving Molly the scone became mine, through, of course, my noisy persistence.

After feeding time, father would lift me in his calloused hands and seat me on Molly's neck and I shrieked with joy! But it was a different tale when it was time for me to dismount and watch father and his mare move off. I wept sorely. I was very closely attached to the pair.

EARLY DEATH

One of the jobs my father liked doing was delivering the barrels of grain whiskey, or strong drink of any kind, which came by rail for Coleraine publicans. And the big fellow could throw those barrels and containers off as he would egg cases, such was his strength and knack.

Each pub would reward him with a glass or two of whiskey and so he mostly came home in the evenings under the influence of drink. He was never aggressive in that state and always saw that we got sufficient clothes and food.

But mother was deeply concerned and hurt about the drinking habit and for the sake of his own health and the future of his children she kept pleading with father to refuse the publicans so-called kind treats. A devout Presbyterian, brought up in a strict temperance family, mother classed whiskey as the devil's liquid. She shuddered at the smell of it.

My father, however, let mother's pleas in one ear and out of the other. He went on drinking until he deteriorated in body and strength. When a pathetic shadow of himself, he had to part from his job and our beloved Molly.

The grain whiskey had taken its toll so eventually father died at an early age leaving his Mary Edith with the responsibility of the rearing of four young children in a lean era that was without the benefit of widows pension or government social security of any kind.

MOTHERS THRIFT

In the case of a working-class widow being unable to find work to support her children or, worse still, a widow being unable to work for her children, the alternative was admittance to a prison-like workhouse, where inmates were tagged paupers, the lowest creatures of the human race.

But Mary Edith Moore was inflicting none of that degrading existence upon her four youngsters. A woman of indomitable courage, on seeing my sisters out to school each morning, she went charring, taking me with her. Only a tiny tot I wasn't happy standing for hours watching her on hands and knees clean and scrub homes and buildings from top to bottom.

Neither was mother happy with having to submit me to such a mostly cold and monotonous daily routine. But it was a case of necessity in the interest of my care and protection. There was just no other way.

Somehow, mother managed to earn sufficient money weekly to pay the rent, keep the home fire burning and though beefsteak breakfasts were unknown to us we had good helpings of porridge oats and pots of soup she made with vegetables got from amateur gardeners and four shin bones bought each week from a family butcher for a penny apiece.

On Sundays we always had spuds and a bowl of buttermilk with the soup so, thankfully, we were fairly well sustained.

It was a jubilant day for us when Aunt Annie Parkhill made mother the gift of a Singer sewing machine. It wasn't a new one, but worked quite well on a foot peddling system.

Mother soon learned to operate the revolutionary invention and began making her daughters petticoats and bloomers out of flour sacks, which were plentiful through housewives baking their own bread on griddle and in oven pot. The sacks, of course, had to be boiled in soap suds in an effort to remove the manufacturer's name and slogans. This was not always possible, but my sisters didn't seem to mind carrying the trade mark of Spillers around with them as long as it wasn't visible to the public. In fact, they made good fun out of it.

Sometimes members of my mother's family circle would give her their left-off clothing from which she fashioned and made frocks and skirts for Etta, Jeannie and Annie and trousers for me. And also being a fast and skilled knitter, mother made sure we were never without a change of warm woollen jerseys.

As well as working hard daily towards our keep, mother also dedicated her spare time to us and, quietly, slipped other families in dire need, petticoats, bloomers, frocks and boys trousers, considering it a labour of love. Her heart was very big and kind.

NEW JOB

Then good fortune decreed that my mother's application for a job in a linen mill directly across the River Bann from Abbey Street, should be successful.

And, mercy be! The excited woman was also allocated a house, beautifully situated overlooking the River Bann, on the Strand Road, beside the mill, with the luxuries of gas lighting in each room and a flushing closet in the back yard. One pull of a chain and human deposits disappeared as if by magic!

In addition, the house, one of a row of six, had a proper front door. It wasn't cut in two like the entrances to many westside homes, and a narrow hall, its floor fitted with red oilcloth the previous tenant had left, led to a small parlour, its walls covered with a cream paper bearing prints of flowers and the floor had a matching square of dark yellow oilcloth - further gifts of the kind former tenant.

The parlour furniture comprised two black horse-hair chairs with bow-shaped legs and a shiny brown table beneath the window, which held a large open Bible and a pot with a plant. Prominent among a number of pictures on the walls was a large one of King William crossing the Boyne on his big white stallion.

My late father had been a staunch orangeman like his great-grandfather, Joshua Moore, his grandfather, William Moore and father, Cochrane Moore, so the picture had been handed down as was the ancient sash in the big tin bandbox, which held other family treasures.

But it must be said that my mother displayed King William's picture for sentimental reasons only. She did not have the slightest essence of sectarian bitterness. Her motto was. "Live and let live."

The next door in the hall led to the kitchen, which had a coke fire between two stone hobs. Mother did the cooking on the fire and the hobs were used as resting places for the frying pan and pots when in use.

Of course we had the gas ring, but it was only used in an emergency, for it cost a penny every two hours of gas it burned and the penny had to be inserted in a meter. Believe me a penny to the poor of long ago was a very very important coin.

Attached to our kitchen was a small scullery with a water tap and sink and apart from washing cooking utensils and dishes there my mother and sisters washed their bodies and legs as best they could, using a large tin bath. Pitifully then, working-class homes didn't have bathrooms of any kind.

On the left of the kitchen entrance was a set of stairs leading up to two bedrooms. Mother and sisters occupied the big front one and I had the small back one, plus a full-sized single bed, all to myself - lucky, lucky boy!

The year was 1915 and 400 women in the mill were weaving a special texture of Irish linen for, it was whispered, the wings of machines that could fly in the air and were to be a force in the war then raging.

The interior of the mill was a busy dusty and noisy daily scene, which mother soon acclimatised herself to. She was always early to begin a 12-hour shift from 6am to 6pm - a conscientious habit not alone to boost the war effort, but to satisfy the thankfulness in her heart at having a roof over her head and the security of a job, even in the humble capacity of a cleaner.

The working day for mother actually began at 5am following a word of prayer and a bite to eat. Then placing emphasis on the needs of Etta, Jeannie, Annie and me, she would carefully search our garments for holes and loose stitches and do the repairs, if any, before packing griddle-baked soda scones with a scrambled egg between them, for our school lunch at 12.30pm, a feast we always craved.

Mother completed her morning duties by cooking and leaving ready our four porridge breakfasts and the permanently scribbled note for Etta which read: "See that the wane sups his stirabout all up." 'Stirabout' was the common name for porridge.

Finally, mother pulled a grey shawl over her head and shoulders, then blowing a kiss to her sleeping wee ones she left quietly for the mill to team up with another cleaner and dear friend named Suzy.

And such was mother's devotion towards Etta, Jeannie, Annie and me, that even during the mill's tea break at 8.15am, her thoughts were with us. It was then a kindly neighbour, Mrs Tillie McGrotty, slipped into our home and got us out of bed and dressed, fed and off to school.

I didn't like this early morning intrusion and justifiably, for I was just two years and six months old. But getting me up was necessary, for I had to go to school with my sisters, a concession the education authorities had granted mother, due to her work situation.

Indeed, a clergyman who once visited the school compared me with a leaf tossed about in a stormy autumn.

Mother didn't like the remark and neither did the school teachers and pupils. They reckoned it a great thing having such a young chick in their midst and they taught me rhymes and songs and claimed me as their mascot.

Eventually they nick-named me "Puss and Boots", for what reason no one knew. And teachers would take liberty away from the usual curriculum and lift me up on to a chair in front of their pupils and I would recite my rhymes and sing my songs.

Mother was pleased that her wee "Puss and Boots" was getting on well with everyone at school and even though of tender years was able to do a bit of entertaining. But the dear woman often conceded to my sisters that during those morning tea-breaks in the mill she kept praying fervently that my school progress would continue and that I would never never be caught in the web of strong drink. She had lost her husband through the curse and didn't want to loose a son the same cruel way.

SLIM BUDGET

My mother's wage for a 66 hour week amounted to ten shillings out of which she paid four shillings a week for rent, leaving her six shillings to feed us. Yet, we were never hungry. The shin bones had been reduced to two a week, for Friday evenings, when mill workers received their pay, called for a fry of forcemeat and onions.

The forcemeat - known as mincemeat today - cost sixpence for a fairly big portion, which also gave us a Saturday meal.

Our next door neighbours, the Duffin family being Catholics, didn't eat meat on Fridays because of a church rule, but they always had the next best thing, Ardglass fresh herrings. And as the two pans sizzled and their odours escaped outside to mix harmoniously like the two families did, lighthearted passers-by were at times prompted to wish us "Sharp appetites" to enjoy our meals.

Amazingly, after mother had got her weeks provisions out of the six shillings and had put threepence in the church envelope, she had usually a shilling left, which went into our footwear fund. She never at any time considered her own needs. The navy blue costume she wore to Sunday worship was her marriage outfit and it was beginning to fade with age. Nevertheless, it was still good enough in her eyes.

But in spite of mother's saving and managing genius, Christmas 1915 looked like being a bleak one for Etta, Jeannie, Annie and me. The slim family budget didn't allow for toys. The pathetic sight of empty stockings on the morning of the great day was going to cause rivers of tears and heartbreak.

Instead of moping over the impoverished situation, mother searched around and didn't give up until she had got a job to coincide with her weekly mill works schedule.

Finishing work in the mill at midday on Saturdays, she spent an hour at home, then walked to the other end of the town to the Northern Constitution newspaper building at Railway Road and on hands and knees scrubbed every department, finishing mostly at nine o'clock in the evening for the sum of a half-crown.

Every prized half-crown (two shillings and sixpence) earned went into the safe custody of Northern Constitution clerk, Miss Henry, until required at the festivities for the toy-buying spree. Was it any wonder the very impressed Miss Henry said on handing over the money: "You are a brave and wonderful person Mary Edith. I just hope the sacrifices you've made for your children are made known to them and that they repay you one day."

Christmas 1915, proved to be a joyous one for us. As we played with our selection of toys, thanking Santa for his generosity, mother sat resting her tired legs on a chair - legs that above the ankles were showing signs of dreaded ulcers, the result of long hours of toil. Irrespective of this, the brave woman was smiling, finding her happiness in ours.

REAL HARDSHIP

Mother's partner at work, Suzy, apart from handling a broom and heavy bins of fibre dust and rubbish, had a hard life with a husband who was fonder of the wine bottle than he was of the six children he had given her in quick succession and without reasonable thought for their future. The money he earned at the docks more often went into the cash box of a publican rather than Suzy's purse.

But that dire neglect didn't stop the little woman from loving her three boys and three girls dearly and she often wept sorely when discussing them with my mother. She wished from the depth of her kind heart that she could give them a better rearing.

Suzy's home in Dunlop Street, near to the mill, isn't difficult to describe - a small kitchen and fireplace and in the area of the backyard an even smaller department where she and her husband and youngest child slept, quite cramped.

At bedtime the other five children, like many of their kind in Dunlop Street, climbed a ladder to a wood loft above the kitchen and somehow got to sleep lying on a chaff palliasse.

Chaff was the remnants of wheat sheafs after the threshing of the seeds and farmers were keen to get rid of it. In quantity it made warm comfortable bedding, but, sadly, was a favourite breeding ground for fleas, a dominating menace in 1915 to big families living in small homes and the west side of the River Bann at Coleraine had many of them.

My mother and I visited Suzy two or three times a week with mother helping her to bath the younger children for bed. The girls had always ample flour sack petticoats and bloomers and the boys well-hemmed trousers, thanks to the Singer sewing machine and my mother's skill in handling it.

Suzy envied our flushing closet and complained bitterly about the dry one in the yard she and her family had to use. Twice a month the container in the closet and its load had to be carried through the kitchen and emptied in a dung cart outside the front door.

When Tom Lamont's horse-drawn cart came to collect, there was a noticeable absence of people about the street. The stink was unbearable.

But back to normality, Dunlop Street was a homely place. Small though the kitchens were, the tenants took pride in them and the brass fenders that shone beneath the bright coke fires.

VIEW FROM THE WINDOW

When the clear evenings of 1916 came my mother, home from work, loved to have a basin of hot water by the window of her bedroom and while easing her swollen feet and ulcerated legs in it she would interest herself in the activities outside.

From mid-April to the end of June, Mayflower blossomed thickly on both Bann shores at Coleraine and my mother was put under its spell as many other observers were. Sadly, the vile river pollution of today denies nature-lovers of this gorgeous spectacle.

And though not a rowing connoisseur, mother, from her window, liked seeing the lithe young men of the Bann Rowing Club, on the other side of the river, come down the steps into a streamlined boat and a couple of minutes later swing their oars as if in response to a single will.

This precise action appealed to me as well, for I was always at mother's side when she was at home. She never tired saying to me: "I pray and hope you grow up to be like those young men."

Mother was, of course, aware that the Bann Rowing Club was strictly temperance and she was fully intent in bringing me up to believe in that virtue.

Chapter
T W O

COLERAINE HAS AN INTERESTING HISTORY GOING BACK FIFTEEN HUNDRED YEARS TO THE TIME OF ST PATRICK, who on coming to the area was offered ground on which to build a church. He chose a spot overgrown with ferns, hence the name Coleraine, which is Anglicised from the Irish Culrathain - Ferny corner.

In 1916 the town, with a population of 7,000, had no electric power of any kind. The streets had a number of tall iron lamp standards with fancy glass lanterns on top and just before darkness each evening a man with a pole came round, reached up, pulled a bracket attached to a lantern down and quite an area was illuminated with bright gaslight. The same operation in putting the lights out was performed at dawn.

There was a lamp standard positioned directly outside our front door at Strand Road and that pleased my mother immensely, for it saved her the expense of using the parlour and upstairs front bedroom lights.

Indeed, our location and gaslight facilities, indoor and outdoor, once inspired philosopher and bookworm, the Reverend Andrew Wilson. On an annual visit to my mother and family, keen members of his flock, the esteemed minister was reminded of a ditty he had learned when a boy and which he recited to us quite dramatically over a cup of tea.

'Tis town yet country too, you feel the warmth,
Of clustery houses in winter time;
Sup with a friend and go by gaslight home.
And hear the tiny bleat of new-weaned lambs.

Yes, we were within range of rural sights and sounds and on the days of mid-summer had the thrill of seeing thousands of salmon jumping non-stop in the River Bann, displaying dazzling flashes of silver and elegant curves. Whether those aerobatics were for the joy of arriving home or to get rid of irritating sea lice, no one could tell. But that caused no concern. All that mattered was they had come back in large numbers.

A mile upstream from our home was the Salmon Leap, a very beautiful stretch of broken water with crystal-like water falls on each side. There, especially at high tide, salmon were seen in sometimes vain, but often successful attempts to surmount the west fall to gain sanctuary in the non-tidal water above. And the failures, undaunted, would return again and again to the encounter with renewed energy until victory was theirs. It was a miracle of strength and sheer determination to behold!

But, alas, many of the gallant silver denizens would take the easier streams between the falls and if they didn't go through the King's Gap to the freedom of the Upper Bann, would finish in the fishery traps, which meant a trip in ice to cross-Channel market slabs - a sad ending after going and coming back thousands of miles in swims fraught with danger.

SCHOOL

The working-class schoolchildren of 1916 didn't have the benefits of school transport, school meals nor school central heating. Killowen National School, which Etta, Jeannie, Annie and I attended, was a big barren building sectioned off in classrooms and any fires or makeshift stoves used in winter absolutely failed to provide sufficient heating, a grim situation not helped with most pupils being ill-clad.

And National Schools in my boyhood, known as Primary Schools today, had no scholarships to assist school leavers with free advanced education. No matter how clever the departing pupil was, he or she in all probability, were destined for an impoverished existence at the docks, in the mill, hiring to a farmer, in a shirt and collar factory or enlistment in the army. The prospect of one of them becoming a member of a profession was nil. Indeed, it was unthinkable!

Killowen Street, joined to Strand Road by two narrow braes, was a long corridor of friendliness. The dwellings, all working-class, varied in shape and size - some roofed with slate, some with tin and some thatched with straw.

Many of the street's young men and not-so-young men were away fighting in the war while most women worked. Even schoolboys from the age of seven to fourteen had jobs before beginning school in the mornings, which helped to keep the hungry wolf from their parent's door.

Most of the boys, from 7am to 9am, delivered milk to homes by means of pint tin cans hung on lengths of strong steel and carried in each hand. It was a system that required considerable care and skill and was appreciated by the recipients, though, compared with today's standard of delivery, it may not not have been one hundred percent hygienic.

FLEA BITES

As I have previously explained in this narrative fleas were a menace in my early boyhood, particularly to those big families lying head to feet on palliasses of chaff. The result was that the pupils sleeping under such cramped conditions brought the cursed insects to school and passed them on to other pupils.

I always had a reasonable share of them and they tore open my tender flesh with their razor-sharp nippers. They were unmerciful!

When my mother got home from work some evenings and saw flea bites on my face and neck, she would immediately strip me and boil my clothes in soap suds and then put me in a hot bath well-treated with disinfectant and my sisters would watch and laugh. Miraculously, they escaped the vicious attacks at school and, according to peat fire logic, it was because of their jet black hair. Me being very fair-haired, I had to suffer.

To people, with a bit of pride, flea bites were degrading and embarrassing. If one of the black marks appeared on their face they never wanted to be seen in public until it had gone and that took two or three days of healing.

Brides-to-be and bridesmaids going to bed each night for their beauty sleep before the day of days, pulled the netting of bacon rolls over their heads, necks and arms for protection, for it was said that one ugly flea bite on a prominent part of a bride or her maid would have caused lots of uneasiness and maybe the postponing of the marriage ceremony.

Indeed, flea bites were responsible for such serious absenteeism at Killowen school that a very concerned teacher, Mistress Thompson, was prompted to give a lecture on the habits of the marauding insect which, she hoped, would counteract any embarrassment caused to the victims of its bites and, more important, bring the pupils back to the classrooms.

After twenty minutes on the platform the teacher concluded with reassuring bounce in her voice: "The tiny lively creatures will only nip healthy boys and girls, so do not let a simple little mark worry you in any way ... it just proves that you are healthy and strong."

But wise old Bob Creary, the chief dispensary doctor, had a different story to tell the staff of the local workhouse two days later. Said he: "The flea, and there are many species, has been recognised as the most dangerous of all insects, for it spreads the Bubonic plague by carrying the germ from rats to humans."

The flea saga finishes on an almost unbelievable note. In the midst of bites and embarrassments a character had the audacity to bring a circus of performing fleas to Coleraine and it was quite amazing with the tiny culprits in a large glass case pulling chariots and doing all kinds of tricks, one being the building of a tower by springing on top of each other. Their reward was a session of blood sucking periodically on the backs of the trainer's hands.

SAD NEIGHBOURS

My mother was friendly with all the tenants of Strand Road row of houses, especially with Annie Duffin, next door to us and, of course, Tillie McGrotty, who got Etta, Jeannie, Annie and me, out to school in the mornings. Tillie lived on the other side of the Duffins.

Mother could enter both homes without knocking. She had trying moments for a time consoling a nervous Annie Duffin, whose husband Jim's battalion had been in the thick of a battle in France and news had filtered through that he was wounded and in a field hospital.

Tillie McGrotty's husband Willie, her sons John, Jimmy and Willie (jun), were also serving in France, so mother, was always rendering a wee bit of comfort to both neighbours and visiting them as often as possible.

Then came the Battle of the Somme in July, 1916, during which thousands of the cream of Ulster youth and men were killed and wounded. Jimmy McGrotty was gunned-down in the advance. Just 22, he had already experienced the horrors of the Dardanelles, came home and was permitted the time only to embrace his loving mother and the younger members of the family, then he was ordered to France and his untimely death.

I do not remember the Somme epic nor the Jimmy McGrotty tragedy, but was informed later that the McGrotty, Duffin and Moore families wept for a solid fortnight. And we were not alone. Every corner of Ulster was weeping with us in grief, such was the mass shedding of the blood of dear ones on foreign soil.

PROMISING POTENTIAL

At the age of five I was enrolled in the infants department of Killowen School and the fact that I was able to say the alphabet without help and count up to 100 was an advantage in beginning my education.

Mother, whose term of education ended when she was twelve, kept teaching me to read simple stories and to add and subtract simple sums and so on the principal, himself, taking the infants one morning and having picked me out for questioning, he afterwards went on to consider my academic potential promising. He dismissed me saying: "Keep your shoulder to the wheel boy and I'll be seeing you in the seventh standard one day."

A junior teacher had told my mother about this and the dear woman bubbled over with delight and kept assuring herself that Wee Willie was going to be a bright scholar. Big men like principals were rarely wrong in their judgments.

And after Etta, Jeannie and Annie, in turn, read a verse from the Bible before going to bed each night, mother would take me to the one side and warn me about the evil of strong drink and the people who seem to get satisfaction from offering it to young folk. I listened carefully and began hating the stuff as my mother hated it. Certainly it would never touch my lips.

DOUBLE BEREAVEMENT

My sister Etta was fourteen, the compulsory age for leaving school. A nice modest girl she got a job in Rogers Shirt and Collar Factory the following Monday and was quite excited about it. At last she could be of some help financially to the wonderful mother who had given so much to the rearing of her and her two sisters and wee brother.

A year later, my sister Jeannie, a lovely girl like Etta, also started work in the Shirt and Collar Factory and the two extra pay packets, though the contents were small, certainly helped the Moore family economy.

But, alas, this progress wasn't to last too long. Etta became ill and to her great disappointment had to take time off work. Later the illness was diagnosed to be the dreadful wasting incurable disease consumption.

After work in the mill my mother sat with Etta, holding the dying girl's hand until the vexed woman's eyes closed and her head fell on the bed in exhaustion. And Jeannie and Annie wouldn't leave. Over-stricken with grief they too sat by their sister's side, watching her face get thinner and thinner and turn like wax.

In a few weeks dear Etta passed on as she had lived, quietly, and as she lay in that downstairs parlour, which was packed with the flowers of sympathisers, there was evidence that death had lifted from her frail shoulders a heavy burden. She no longer looked tired.

Some months later, tragedy was to strike at our family again. Dear Jeannie also became a victim of consumption and after suffering its awful wasting torture, joined Etta.

As history will reveal, unknown to the authorities in the late teens and early twenties of the last century there were herds of milking cows with tuberculosis with the sad result that men and women and boys and girls died, the victims of consumption.

The great double loss of Etta and Jeannie in the course of such a short time caused widespread shock and sorrow. It was thought my mother would crumble under the strain. But her courage remained firm. She had to continue on for the sake of her other two young children - praise God that she got keeping them.

I was feeling weary about my big sisters departure, leaving just Annie and me. Gone was Etta and Jeannie's affection and gone was the good fun they created and home was not the same without them. It was a terrible terrible lonely place.

One day I was weeping sorely for my sisters and as I stood by the river side along came a preacher, a friend of our family.

Lifting me on to the Bann wall he said: "You must be brave and accept the ways of God in Heaven, where, if we're good, we will go one day." Then the preacher smiled and went on in heartsome tone: "God needed two special angels for his Heaven, so He chose Etta and Jeannie and called them."

That night in bed I kept pondering over what the preacher had told me and recalled Etta and Jeannie speak about angels as they read their Bibles. Now they were two angels themselves and in my mind's eye I could see them in white silk shining robes and great wings. In my innocence I got to sleep hoping that they would fly down soon and see mother, Annie and me.

WHIPPING

Living so close to the River Bann it was only natural that I should become a fisherman at an early age. I used a 10ft hazel sapling for a rod and the line was a length of cord.

It was the merry month of May and shoals of little silver fish named 'cuttings' had come to Coleraine from the sea and they were fond of a piece of bread pressed on a small hook. There were many of them in a burn meandering through Camerons Marsh, directly opposite Killowen School.

This induced me to take my rod to school and leave it in the porch and on the ringing of the lunch bell at 12.30pm I would go hunting the 'cuttings' in Camerons burn.

I always had my soda scone and scrambled egg nibbled away at the arrival of the lunch half-hour with the exception of a crumb or two I had kept for bait, so there was no time wasted.

One of those lunch half-hours I will remember until my last breath on earth. As usual I had left my slippers under the desk, picked up my rod, and, barefoot, went fishing.

Any 'cuttings' I caught I put back in the burn and when the 12.55pm bell rang to return to lessons I had thoroughly enjoyed the outing.

Coming up the marsh I climbed the fence and with rod over my shoulder stood waiting on the side of the road to let a pony and trap pass. A lady and gentleman were the occupants of the trap.

Unfortunately, when the pony came in line with me it seemed to get scared, for it lifted its front legs high a couple of times. However, when it settled seconds later I continued my journey across the road to the school. But going through the gate entrance I heard a shout behind me.

Turning round I saw the gentleman from the trap. His eyes burned with anger and he carried a whip! Raising it high he brought the stinging lash down on my right ear and shoulder and thinking the ear was cut off my head I began screaming!

The next attack was on my neck and shoulders. Then knocking me to the ground with his fist he continued to whip me on the bare legs and body and kept doing so incessantly until the principal came. By that time I lay still in a dazed state.

The intruder to the school playgrounds' excuse for the brutal assault was that I had frightened his young blood pony by waving my fishing rod as it passed.

To my knowledge I didn't wave the rod and there were witnesses to prove it. But, dear God! Even if I had, punishment should have been placed in the hands of the principal instead of me being left with a mass of ugly purple scars and almost senseless to the world.

My mother, distraught at the nasty occurrence and the pathetic sight of me, went in search of a Guardian of Workhouse Affairs and the Poor Law System, from whom a sick line had to be obtained for the authorisation of a doctor to come and see me.

At last this awful red tape, dealing with the lives of human beings, was sorted and so a doctor, complete with Gladstone bag arrived at our home to see me the evening after the whipping.

Studying my injuries over the top of small wire specs, the medical man announced his cure to my mother: "Keep bathing in hot water and time will heal."

In the days that followed, the pain of the scars was agony and my mother was afraid that serious complications would set in. The doctor never came back and mother didn't complain, for she had little faith in him. Her mainstay was continuous prayer.

Mother wept bitterly when she heard the name of the culprit who gave me the whipping - Sir Ronald Hervey Bruce. She kept asking herself the question: "How could he have caused her wee son such injuries and pain and, seemingly, get away with it?"

Many kindly Killowen folk, who visited me were furious with the titled attacker. Their sympathy towards me and keenness for justice resulted in a sum of money being collected to enable my mother to take time off work to attend to legal matters in connection with the whipping.

Next day she went to the police and told them that public opinion was that they should take a case against the person who so brutally attacked her wee son.

The head constable's reply was: "You're son didn't get the whipping for nothing."

And a solicitor's answer to my mother when she asked about the possibility of taking court action was: "Go home woman and forget about it ... you would only be running your head against a stone wall."

On her way back to the Strand Road my tearful mother confirmed the view of working-class folk that there was a law for the rich and one for the poor.

Sir Ronald Hervey Bruce was the fifth baronet of Downhill. The general saying was that if my father had been alive and in his prime he would have taken the law into his own hands and severely punished my attacker, irrespective of the consequences.

Sometime after the whipping the baronet moved from Northern Ireland to Eastbourne, England, where he was killed in an accident thus described in a leading English daily newspaper: "Suffered a fatal fall from the Marine Parade during a particularly spectacular thunder storm."

A hasty death the Moore family in no way wished him.

Chapter
THREE

AT THE AGE OF SEVEN YEARS AND FOUR MONTHS ANY
ENTHUSIASM I HAD FOR LEARNING HAD COMPLETELY
gone. As my Aunt Mary Jane Moore termed the situation: "I was in
a rut" and mother in agreeing was furious. I had let the confidence
the principal had in me down.

Somehow I had managed to edge myself into the third standard
before the rut had set in. There the desks were arranged in a system
of merit - the smart pupils to the fore and the not-so-smart ones to
the rear.

The desk I shared was one from the bottom. Having gone
beyond mother's teaching ability my homework was sometimes in
such a shambles that I was punished on the flats of both hands with
slaps from the teacher's cane and they hurt. And I wasn't too well
behaved neither in classroom nor playground, through, perhaps, being
spoiled a bit during those early 'Puss and Boot' years.

I was the fighting type and that was necessary, for there were a
few bullies around. If a boy submitted to their demands and threats

he was continually intimidated. But a boy who bravely stood up and had a real fistic 'go' with them was never troubled afterwards, for they were cowards at the bottom. I discovered that a few times.

Speaking truthfully, I had come to hate school. To me it had become a place I wanted out of, even though it was seven years before I could leave. Seven long horrible years!

I was much more interested in selling Coleraine Chronicles on Friday afternoons and mother had permitted me to do that job with the warning; "Wherever you go keep away from bad company." She was worried about me going out on my own. But as Tillie McGrotty wisely said to her: "Your boy has got to leave your apron strings at sometime, especially if the calling is a commercial one."

In that era the Chronicle consisted of four broad sheets and cost a penny. I was getting rid of two dozen, which allowed me sixpence commission and the moving around was also showing me some of the ways of the world.

For instance I will never forget the spring afternoon I approached a tall silver-haired gentleman, Bob O'Neill, a local solicitor, with my bunch of papers under my arm and said: "Please sir, would you like to buy a Chronicle?"

The gentleman stopped on his step, put his hand in his pocket and withdrawing sixpence replied: "I get the Chronicle delivered at my home, but for your mannerly approach and proper address please accept this little reward."

A silver sixpence? It was a fortune! And Mr O'Neill's kindly act taught me that politeness, which costs nothing, pays dividends in whatever transactions one indulges in.

That particular Friday evening I felt like a man handing my mother eleven pence instead of the usual five pence, but though she appreciated the gesture, she didn't hesitate to let me know that she would be much happier if I paid more attention to my education and emphasised that it was vital to my future.

LOYAL JIMMY

My desk partner in the third standard was a boy, aged ten and nicknamed Loyal Jimmy, because of his bitterness towards

Catholics. His low standard and desk status would suggest that he was dull and lackadaisical. Nothing of the kind. He was as old-fashioned as Methuselah, himself. Like me, he just didn't want to learn.

Mistress McDermott was our teacher and Loyal Jimmy at times wasn't too kind to her. She would, maybe, have been in the middle of an important lesson when he interrupted with a silly question and had a little laughing session to himself.

But the strict teacher in no way was accepting this tomfoolery and so she would bring the culprit up in front of the class and punish him severely with her cane. And those slaps could have been on top of a couple he had already received for failing at sums and reading.

The big bad boy had a notion that his interruption of lessons and holding out his hand for punishment 'lifted' him in the eyes of his fellow pupils. He was wrong, for though just youngsters we had the sense to know that those classroom acts were an endeavour to conceal his inferiority complex and, when that came to the fore he would give me some awful slaggings at the desk. He called me a "show-off" and a "swank" for having a room and a bed all to myself, a parlour, a gasring and flushing closet.

I just listened to my enraged desk partner and kept my mouth shut. I was never angry at his insulting attacks. On the contrary, I was sympathetic towards him when I thought of his awful existence in a one room thatch cabin at Burnside on the Screen Road, which was without water and sanitary facilities. And his sleeping quarters, with seven brothers and sisters, was a makeshift outhouse, while his father and mother, Alex and Gemima, occupied the mud-floor cabin.

Alex and Gemima were assessed by the Killowen and Coleraine communities as having King William on the brain. They actually worshipped and cheered a colourful picture of the monarch above their bed, keeping enough breath to publicly give the fenians a rough touch of their tongues.

And in spite of the smallness of the thatch roof of their cabin, the obsessed couple always found space during each July, to fly a Union Jack and orange and purple flags to commemorate King William's Boyne victory, with another Union Jack on the top of the children's sleeping quarters.

Loyal Jimmy was following closely in his parents staunch footsteps. He knew all the party songs off by heart and would start singing them wherever there were people. From the start of each spring every day was a miniature 'Twelfth' to the young red, white and blue fanatic. But that noisy activity also helped to subdue his inferiority complex of which, we knew, he was continually conscious.

BOYNE FEVER GRIPS ME

On strictly lecturing me from time to time on the evils of alcoholic drinks and bad company, my mother would bring up another subject 'sectarianism' which prevailed strongly locally, particularly in the weeks leading to July 12th.

Waving that reproving finger she would advise: "You can be loyal to your Protestant beliefs and certainly spectate at a 'Twelfth', but never never get hatred and bitterness in your heart against people who are not Protestants. It is not Christian. And remember that while I am the ruling power over you."

I was in a predicament. Dear mother wanted me to be non-sectarian minded and the Killowen School pupils expected me to be like them, full of the 'Boyne fever' as the season of marching feet and battering of drums approached.

In the playground at lunchbreak they kept praising glorious King Billy and running down Catholics in phrases that were anything but polite. They were quite fanatical!

And when Loyal Jimmy wasn't slagging me at the desk he took the liberty to teach me party songs and in no way did I try to close my ears to his efforts. Already I could sing 'Derrys Walls' and 'The Sash My Father Wore'. And why shouldn't I sing that lively song? Didn't my father wear the sash of his great-grandfather, grandfather and father and it was still in the bandbox waiting for me to wear when I became of age.

I vividly recall one day at the desk when Loyal Jimmy was denouncing Catholics he said: "If you let them on top they'll run over you and destroy you. We've got to keep fighting them and uphold our rights to live freely under the Crown."

Even though I wasn't the brightest of pupils I found such patriotism difficult to understand from a boy who slept on the floor of a hovel, used the back of a hedge for a toilet, quenched his thirst in a spring burn the cattle used and walked to school barefoot for most of the year. Nevertheless, his song teaching and daily spasms in the defence of Protestantism on top of the pupils enthusiasm smit me and so I contracted 'Boyne fever'.

Much as I loved my mother and respected her rules I just couldn't be the odd boy out at Killowen School. I had joined the pupils in their biased playground demonstrations and soon became one of the main advocates of bitterness.

My chest bulged with pride at the compliments my loyal stand was receiving. I met Loyal Jimmy's father Alex one day and patting me on the back he said: "You're a real good one ... keep the colours flying high." Then taking my hand in a firm grip he added: "You bear the great Christian name of William, the same name as our illustrious Royal Sovereign. Be proud of it son wherever you go in the world."

I had one big problem in my new loyal routine and that was keeping the members of the Catholic Duffin family, next door neighbours, at a distance. Our back yards were separated only by a couple of strands of wire and Jim Duffin, not long discharged from the army, would sit there smoking a cigarette and, probably, reflecting on the tough battles he had taken part in.

When he was in the yard I remained indoors to avoid chatting with him. And if my mother sent me to the yard for something and he spoke to me as he always did, I would either pretend not to have heard him or answer abruptly and hasten indoors.

Of course, my mother wasn't aware of my biased conduct towards Jim Duffin and family and I made doubly sure she didn't find out knowing well that if she had, not only would I have been severely chastised, it would have caused her hurt and embarrassment in the friendly and peaceful neighbourhood we lived in and where she was highly regarded.

But I carried on with my bitter change of heart and enjoyed it. Since Alex's boost, my name William had become an endearing part of me and I got it into my head that my father was called for the King of Kings and the honour was now mine.

I had added 'Dolly's Braes' and 'The Siege' to my repertoire and after singing them never failed to loudly herald the hero's slogan, No Surrender! I was fanatically pledged and addicted to the cause of Derry, Aughrim, Enniskillen and the Boyne.

But in spite of me trying to keep the Duffin family at a distance I got into a fix one unforgettable day I just couldn't get out of. I was doing something at the upper end of our back yard when Annie Duffin, Jim's wife, and a young daughter Kathleen, came out to their yard weeping. They had lost a wee son and brother and were demonstrating the loss sorely, the very pretty daughter in her mother's arms.

After a few minutes Annie, dressed in black and whose face was pathetically pale and tear-stained, came to the fence and said to me in broken voice: "Willie son, would you like to come in and say farewell to Terry before they put the lid on his coffin?"

I shuffled about for a moment wondering what to do. Then I recalled the Duffin family being the first sympathisers in our house to comfort my mother when sisters Etta and Jeannie had died. In the next few seconds I was following the mother and daughter into the bereaved home.

From the back door I could see the little boy in his white coffin, which was laid on two chairs in the corner of the kitchen and truly he looked like a beautiful angel. Tears filled my eyes and the feeling of bitterness left my young heart as I envisaged Terry in the company of Etta and Jeannie in Heaven.

Someone then ushered my small frame into a queue of weeping children and when it came my turn I bent over the coffin and kissed Terry on the forehead as the children were doing.

But all this was too much for me and when I left the Duffin home I went to my bedroom where I shed more tears and began thinking - Yes, it was sad ... very sad. Still, I could never tell my friends at school that I had kissed a Catholic - even one God had called.

THE TWELFTH

Many Killowen people were employed in the linen mill and being predominantly Protestant, they had voted that the annual two days holiday coincided with the 12th and 13th of July, the 12th to enable them to take part in or attend the demonstrations and the 13th to go to Portrush or Portstewart to relax and bathe tired feet in the cool of the briny sea.

The evening of July 11th was also a time of much rejoicing in Killowen under the arches and colourful banners and bunting and flags. And every fifty yards was a bonfire with instrumentalists round them playing suitable music and creating happiness.

On one particular 11th July evening my enthusiasm had developed into sheer frenzy. I had forgotten about everything only the exciting hours ahead. My mother had allowed me to stay up late with the promise that she would take me to the Killowen celebrations.

At last the time was approaching for our departure to the bright lights, music, singing and dancing. Mother had just a few dishes to wash and then we were off. While patiently waiting mother's exit from the kitchen sink I went into the parlour and began appraising King William's picture and on finishing blew him a kiss.

If it had not been for him there would be no celebrations in Killowen tonight and no 'Twelfth' demonstrations tomorrow. I shuddered at the thought! Alex and Gemima were quite right to worship His Majesty.

I had no need to be awakened on the 12th morning. I was up like a lark and away to kiss and hug my mother. It was her birthday and though I was sincere the occasion was secondary to the demonstration later in the morning. And mother didn't mind, for she had long since treated birthdays as just another year older.

The big demonstration was being held in Limavady and I was going there in the company of Suzy and her three sons and three daughters. who would be wearing the little orange sashes their mother had somehow found time to make.

I had hoped that Suzy would have made me a sash. She didn't. But not to worry, I had a good substitute for the breast of my dark blue velvet suit in a freshly plucked giant orange lily and a purple rocket. They would serve my strong loyal ego well.

I didn't have to be coaxed into the big tin bath that memorable morning. Neither did I object to a double scrubbing and sponging, ears and all, with finger and toe nails cut and filed. The special preparation had to be the heights of perfection to honour the gallant

Billy's Boyne victory. Oh what a wonderful feeling it was to be a Protestant on the morning of the glorious 'Twelfth'!

When dressed with the giant orange lily and purple rocket added to my attire, I looked like a new pin. Even the miniature Union Jack I carried toned splendidly with my velvet suit and mother had to admit that she had taken a second notion of me.

Then on my fond-doting mother putting the train fare to Limavady in my trouser pocket for Suzy's attention, she searched the bottom of her purse and finding four pennies there reached them to me for spending on my day out.

After another kiss and hug and a plea from mother to be a good boy and cause Suzy no trouble, for she would have enough of it with her own over-enthusiastic patriots, I left.

But my short journey to Suzy and family at Dunlop Street was interrupted when Jim Duffin, standing at his front door called me over and slipped a coin into my hand with the words: "That's from the Duffin family ... have a nice day."

Going up the wee brae I peeped at the coin and could hardly believe my eyes. It was a shining silver shilling! What a day I was going to have in Limavady with money left to spend in the Port tomorrow.

In the excitement of the moment tears flowed down my cheeks and as I brushed them away I wished that the Duffin family were Protestants - even quiet ones.

RR STEEL'S MAGIC

Killowen children were back at school after summer holidays and considerable calm had been restored. It was coming the turn of the benign and gracious Santa Claus's time for discussion.

It was also the time for forming the junior and senior pupils for carol singing and that gave Mistress Thompson the opportunity to select the best of them for her choirs. which never failed to compete at Coleraine Music Festival each March with tremendous success.

I was picked for the junior Festival Choir and pupils big and small were of the opinion that the teacher's sense of pity for my whipping got me a spot in the front row. But they had another shock when my voice was considered suitable for the Boys Junior Solo Contest.

Ironically the test piece was named 'Billy Boy'. But it had no connection with the Boyne Billy. It was a simple folk song which I learned quickly and sang with the lilt that was required.

According to my delighted mother I would have to look the part on the big stage of the Town Hall, so my dark blue velvet suit was out of the question. It was now too tight for my growing frame and too childish. I had to have a change.

However, funds were needed for a fashionable boys suit and a shirt with the new style collar attached and a tie. Those items were going to cost quite a bit of money. Again mother came to the rescue by scrubbing out a building in Waterside, which had been converted into a block of offices to let. She completed the job in three evenings after her mill work with Annie and me teaming up to empty the dirty water and fetching the clean. In spite of her cough and ulcerated legs mother seemed inexhaustible.

What a joyous time it was the Saturday afternoon mother and I crossed the bridge to Coleraine shopping centre and purchased the hard earned boys suit, shirt and tie for the sale price of eight shillings and ninepence with the kindly shopkeeper slipping me a 'luck penny' of twopence. Going home I was completely 'over the moon!'

I went to Sunday School very voluntary the next morning dressed in my new outfit and proudly pushed myself past the other children to get sitting beside the teacher. Eventually the lady paid compliment to my new suit, but not without adding with emphasis: "I trust your enthusiasm to sit beside me continues and that you take in what I teach."

Out of a large number of competitors in the Junior Boys Solo at the music festival I gained third place which was to make me the target of Killowen concert promoters. I liked singing and doing actions on platforms, especially if my mother was present.

Sadly the long working hours and the fibre dust were beginning to tell on the dear woman. She had a permanent hoarse cough and those leg ulcers had deepened and not only were they painful, but oozing puss.

Sister Annie always had hot water and the big tin bath ready for mother coming out of the mill so that she could bath the ulcers and try getting the puss out of them. Horrible dark purplish sores they frightened Annie and me and had us weeping at times.

On finishing bathing, mother would wash the rags which acted as bandages for her legs at work and dry them at the fire. Wrapping them round the sores was yet another essential duty she now had to undertake each morning before leaving for the mill. The rags under her stockings, of course, made her legs horribly fat and shapeless. But, fortunately, the long skirts of those years hid them.

It was actually degrading and inhuman some of the things working-class folk had to bear in the course of their humble existence. Mother's evening and morning duties attending to her legs would have shocked the guardians of today's Health Schemes to the core! And she was not alone with those annoying ailments. Suzy and other women in the mill suffered from them.

Medical aid for workers in the mill was either woefully lacking or non-existent, for there was never any help rendered to those ailing women. And if they had taken a forenoon off with the hope of seeing a dispensary doctor their wages were drastically cut, so they just had to slave on and suffer day in and day out. Who ever had the audacity to call them "Good old days?"

Through the medium of our caring clergyman news reached my mother that a Dr Steel, of Castlerock, had a cure for leg ulcers. But to see the busy man and losing a day off work, plus the return train fare to Castlerock and the medical fee, made such an appointment an impossibility. Poor mother could only dream about seeing Dr Steel and pray that a miracle would make it come true one day soon.

Thanks to God Almighty a miracle did happen. On mother coming from work one evening, Annie handed her a long envelope which the postman had delivered that morning. It was a letter from mother's young brother Willie in America and it contained ten dollars with his love.

Ten dollars! That princely sum amounted to £2.40 pennies in English money - more than a month's wages in the mill. A visit to Dr Steel had become a reality to the delight of mother and the ailing women in the mill.

The forenoon mother was going to Castlerock with everyones blessing and best wishes, I was full of excitement, for I was going with her on my first ever visit to the resort. What a thrill it was going to be crossing the River Bann wooden railway bridge!

Arriving in the County Derry paradise, mother showed me the lovely strand leading up to the notorious Barmouth, then named "the grave yard of ships" and other places of interest. Then we went to Dr Steel's residence for the big test.

Mother, who looked nervous, positioned me by a pond with fancy ducks swimming about. Then kissing me she left for the doctor's surgery and I tended to follow her limping form than take an interest in the ducks. God, please look after her.

And tears and anxiety were added to my shaky state as I heard squeals come from the surgery at times. I grabbed a nearby rail tightly and tried to suffer with mother. It was then a disturbing thing entered my mind. I had lost my father and two lovely sisters, now was I going to lose my precious mother?

I stood there, my eyes glued on the door of that Castlerock residence, expecting to see my mother carried out. But, thankfully, she eventually appeared accompanied by the doctor and she was supporting herself and actually smiling.

Giving a big sigh of relief I rushed over to mother and while hugging her learned that the doctor had to be cruel to be kind. He had cleaned the ulcer sores with a fine wire brush before applying his special ointment. This may sound quite unbelievable, but records and indeed, folk still alive, will prove my statement authentic.

Amazingly, mother's ugly ulcers completely dried and healed, so she began a new lease of life in the mill. And dear Suzy's ulcers and the other mill womens were cured by the ageing Dr Steel, whose name became a household word in Killowen.

Chapter FOUR

HAVING A NICE SUIT, SHIRT AND TIE, AT MY DISPOSAL, MOTHER THOUGHT IT WOULD BE GOOD FOR ME IF I joined the Second Coleraine Company of the Boys Brigade, which was run in connection with the three local Presbyterian Churches and was truly a Christian body with a Sunday afternoon Bible Class.

I was no longer sitting beside the teacher in Sunday School nor listening to anything she said. In fact the class had returned to being a bore to me and I was present only because of mother's strict orders. While there my thoughts were in other places - down the river fishing, kicking football in Killowen, swimming along the Sandy Point, gathering dulse and winkles from Portstewart rocks and the Misses McCaws orchard when their big red apples were ripe and sweet.

Now in addition to Sunday School and morning church directly after it, evening church and the Society Street Mission directly after it, mother wanted me to become a member of the the Boys Brigade Bible Class at 3pm each Sunday. Was she trying to make a theological slave of me?

However, I enrolled in the ranks of the brigade and must say that contrary to what I expected I enjoyed the comradeship, learning to drill and march and, particularly, the Sunday afternoon Bible Class.

The class was conducted by an honorary captain, Sam Henry, who had the knack of making each meeting one the boys looked forward to attending.

He was not only a very special teacher of the Scriptures, but one of Ireland's most gifted and cultured men. A native of Coleraine, he was a well-informed student of many subjects including Ulster genealogy and archeology and as a lecturer and writer of them he occupied a pre-eminent place in the community. A leading authority on Irish folk lore he was the discoverer of hundreds of old ballads.

Having this personality each Sunday afternoon with his interesting message and violin and penny whistle, which he played expertly, was a real joy. What a contrast the evening service was in one of the three churches. I just couldn't understand the black -robed figure in the pulpit. Yet if I lifted my eyes off him for a second I got elbow pokes in my sides from mother and sister Annie. Believe me the singing of the last hymn was the only part of those services I enjoyed.

But, alas, much as I liked the Boys Brigade and its Bible Class I was in no way living up to the principals expected of members. And I was also letting my mother down badly. I was stealing apples from the Misses McCaws orchard and in a most organised manner which seemed to make me feel bigger in my slippers rather than a guilty culprit. And, sadly, I was possessed of the notion that a stolen apple was much sweeter than a bought one.

My partners in crime were two big strong senior pupils named Eddie and Joe and their method of getting me on top of the high orchard wall was genius itself. They had pinched a tall flag pole from somewhere so tying a rope tight round my stomach they attached the pole to the rope and lifted my light frame upwards. When on top of the wall I merely climbed down an apple tree to the ground and commenced filling a sack with the big red beauties. Then, tying the neck of the sack I gave the rope a tug and Eddie and Joe started pulling. It was all so easy.

But one afternoon things went terribly wrong. Descending the apple tree with sack and rope I finished in the arms of the big gardener and he wasn't a bit gentle.

That evening, my face as white as a ghost and crying my eyes out, I was handed to my mother by police sergeant, Sam Henderson, who informed the upset woman that Misses McCaw wasn't going to take court action, but that in future her boy was to come to them and ask for apples instead of degrading himself by stealing them.

My chief worry was that the sergeant would tell his son Robin about the theft, for he was an officer in the Boys Brigade. Pathetically I looked up at the towering figure making my appeal. I wanted so much to remain in the ranks.

The sergeant, whose face was showing the glimmer of a smile, replied: "I won't tell Robin if you promise your mother and me that you won't steal any more apples or touch anything that doesn't belong to you?"

Bowing my head I promised faithfully to be good in future and never, never, would I steal another thing. Then the sergeant made his departure leaving me at the mercy of an angry tigress.

I was immediately stripped of every stitch of clothing and hounded upstairs to my bedroom where I was called a "low thief" and "let down" and severely chastised. Then after a couple of hefty slaps on the backside I was put to bed naked! Never had I seen my mother in such temper. She was certainly proving that she was still the boss.

As I lay there bellowing in disgrace I realised that in future I would have to think twice before doing what others told me. I was learning the hard way.

To my surprise and embarrassment, Sam Henry invited me into a small private room after the following Sunday's Bible Class, where he mentioned my apple theft, but not unkindly.

Smiling he said: "You've had a little adventure William since we met last Sunday?" Then he went on more seriously: "You are a small boy full of vigour which you try to get rid of in different ways. You let temptation sway you to the wrong side incited to do so by older boys. It was a flash in the pan, William! Now it's all over. God and everyone forgives you. You are back on the straight road - keep on it boy, it's the only way forward."

Mother and I soon became friends again and it was just great to see the change Dr Steel's magic had made in her way of living. Her legs had become shapely again and there wasn't an ounce of flab on her body, which was easy to understand. She had quite, daringly, shortened the skirt of her costume to above the balls of the legs and had it dyed a lighter blue at the Waterside's revolutionary plant and the years-old costume looked like new.

Mother made sure she was early at the Brigade's Annual Inspection and her face was beaming as she picked one of the chairs lined around the hall. I was watching her from behind a curtain and was fully determined to give a good display in the drill squad, for the guilt of my apple theft and the hurt it had caused her was still inside me.

The inspection went well with every boy trying to excel in front of his parents. A striking and precise performance was the mass march past of platoons. Passing mother with arms swinging and chest out I made sure I was in step. But not to worry really. If I had been out of step the devoted parent would have argued that all the other boys were out of step with her wee Willie ... yes, every one of them!

Through lack of funds I missed the Brigade Summer Camp that year, but had begun saving for the next one and had got another job each Saturday driving a mare named Jill and her buttermilk cart as well as my Chronicle one on Friday afternoons. The pay was four pennies and they went straight into my savings box which, wisely, was in mother's custody.

MUSICIAN

I was continuing with the concert singing and my services were now in demand in places beyond Killowen. But it was in Killowen Parish Church Parochial Hall that something lovely happened to me.

Through a mere incident, due to curiosity, I was to have a new interest which brought much joy into my life's journey and the lives of other people. During the interval of a Mothers Union Concert, I lifted another artiste's mandolin and ran my fingers over the strings.

Then the owner of the mandolin, the unforgettable Tom McDermott, kindly showed me a scale and by the time the concert resumed I was able to play that scale and plectrum it, which

Tom considered to be quite good and reckoned I was a 'natural' for learning the instrument.

At the end of the concert, Tom kindly suggested lending me a spare mandolin he had and so after a few lessons from him I progressed rapidly.

The first two tunes I learned were 'Derry's Walls' and 'The Sash My Father Wore' and, fittingly, I could sing the words and accompany myself on the mandolin. A sixpenny tutor taught me other scales and eventually I became quite accomplished, which Mistress Thompson said was an achievement for a nine-year old boy. Oh! If only I would give the same time and ego to my school lessons.

While mother was delighted that I now played the mandolin, she was afraid that when I strummed 'Derry's Walls' and 'The Sash' I would offend the Duffins, so she kept telling me to keep the sound low. And, hypocritically, I did keep the sound low, for I didn't want to spoil myself of a shilling next 'Twelfth'.

But the 'Boyne fever' was still in my body just waiting to be aroused and I longed for the day when I became the age to wear the sash of my great-great grandfather, Joshua Moore, my great-grandfather, William Moore, my grandfather, Cochrane Moore and my father, William Moore. The relic continued to Lie in State in the big bandbox waiting on the next of kin to carry on the loyal tradition - bless its faded silk and every emblem.

IN MOURNING

Well, the glorious 'Twelfth' did come around again with its usual marching, music and colour, and it was held in Coleraine, with each lodge being led by a band, a big banner and two brethren in black striped trousers, frock coats and tall hats.

And the Duffin family's gift to me that morning was breathtaking - a large silver florin! Two full shillings or, better still, twenty four pennies with no train fare to pay. That was going to greatly help my Boys Brigade camp money!

But, alas, that 'Twelfth' in Coleraine had its big surprise and shock. In fact, Killowen Protestants were dumb struck, for the loyalist fanatics, Alex and Gemima, their son Loyal Jimmy and his six brothers and sisters had not been present at the Killowen 11th night celebrations nor the big demonstration itself. They were nowhere to be seen. Heavens above! What had happened?

Then the disturbing news came from the fortified flagless cabin at Burnside that Lizzie, the eldest daughter of Alex and Gemima, had absconded to Liverpool with a Catholic from Swatragh and married him in a Chapel there.

There could be no celebrating or demonstrating while the devastated family were in full mourning. No, no, a thousand times no!

CAMPING AT BALLYCASTLE

I am keen to describe the ten days camping holiday I had with the Boys Brigade, through mother's goodness. Making sacrifice after sacrifice she made it possible for me to have ten days by the sea, the first time I was ever away from home and really a miracle experience for a boy living in the throes of poverty.

The annual camp was always held at Castlerock, but this year we were going to a place with a popular reputation called Ballycastle, far away on the North Antrim coast and our excitement was tense. And it had a right to be, for apart from the popular venue, we were going there on two charabancs.

Patriotically I made sure I got aboard the charabanc 'Kitty of Coleraine' and the big red coach with a canvas hood when required, chugged along at a speed which sometimes reached an incredible 30 miles an hour when Jamie Lyons, the owner-driver, put the boot down to give us a real thrill.

In addition to my kitbag I had Tom McDermott's mandolin and enroute there was a good vocal response to my playing of such favourites as 'Tipperary' 'Pack Up Your Troubles' and 'Keep The Home Fires Burning'. It was enjoyment at its best.

My first ever sea voyage took place when Sam Henry took a party of volunteers across to Rathlin Island and showed us the cave where the 'try again' spider prompted fugitive Robert the Bruce to return to Scotland, reform his army and gain victory over the English at the Battle of Bannockburn, which ultimately secured Scottish independence.

And Sam told us all about Marconi, the Italian electrical engineer who, some years before, had linked Ballycastle and Rathlin, a distance of eight miles, by wireless.

The ruins of Bonamargy Franciscan Friary were just a short distance from the camp and during a visit to there our learned honorary officer explained that when the Franciscans were forced to leave the friary they buried their alter plate and other valuables in the ground and were never able to come back to recover them.

He also showed us a grave of paramount interest, that of Sorely Boy McDonnell, a powerful and turbulent Scottish-Irish chieftain of the Elizabethan reign, who married for the second time at the age of eighty and had another family.

Visiting time at the camp was a very special Thursday afternoon when parents came to spend a few hours with their sons in the true holiday environment. And they too had the thrill of travelling to Ballycastle on the 'Kitty of Coleraine'.

My mother had somehow managed to take a day off work to come on the first holiday outing of her married and widowed spans and she was a picture in her new-look dyed costume. It was a most wonderful day she later told Suzy at work, especially the hour she and wee Willie strolled along the golden sands hand in hand.

Part of my last day at camp was spent sitting on the green banks of the River Margy strumming the mandolin to the one and only Sam Henry's violin and penny whistle as they sent out to the world his latest discoveries 'The Oul Lammas Fair' and 'If I Were A Blackbird'.

Sam and I became close friends during his long life and I was to learn much from him. I was exceptionally pleased in 1991 when a book containing 700 old Irish songs, discovered by Sam Henry, was published in the U.S.A. by the University of Georgia Press. Entitled 'Songs of the People' the giant book was edited by Gale Huntington, assisted by John Moulden.

MICK THE BUTTERMILK MAN

Buttermilk, the remains of the milk after the butter had been churned from it, was a special mainstay to working-class people following the first world war. It was used for making soda scones on a griddle and was a favourite wash-down for such meals as spuds in their jackets with a slice of dried ling, spuds made into champ mixed with scallions or just spuds and butter if, of course, a bit of butter could have been spared.

Our family weekly supply of buttermilk came from Mick, who drove his mare Jill and dray cart into Killowen on Saturday mornings and reached mother about midday, the time she finished work in the mill.

Mick was the salesman and deliverer for a number of small farmers in the Garvagh district, who appreciated their meagre incomes being strengthened a little by his weekly effort. And, of course, the service in wind, rain, hale and snow, was also appreciated by the customers.

The buttermilk man was my hero and I was very pleased and proud to be his right-hand man. Each Saturday morning I would meet him and his roan mare Jill at the Castle Roe Road - Screen Road corner, a mile from Killowen Street, and jump on the front left side of the cart opposite Mick. Then after a word of greeting I was thrown the reins.

Didn't I feel big at that moment. If one of the new Rolls Royce cars had been put at my disposal I wouldn't have been more thrilled than when I became captain of Mick's yoke and was being paid four pennies.

Feeling the strange touch of the reins Jill would lift her tail high and cock her ears which, probably, were acts of protest against novice dictation, for she required neither rein nor driver. She knew every inch of the road she had trod for years and also knew every one of her master's stops.

Mick was a bent-over little man, who sported an enormous grey moustache which partly concealed the bowl of a clay pipe that never left his mouth except to insert a fill of the strong tobacco he smoked.

His face was a mass of brown wrinkles and his eyes were blue and observant. He wore a battered hat which allowed tiffs of grey hair to escape at places and most important of all he claimed Garvagh breeding through and through and proved it with his keen sense of humour, quick temperament and acts of kindness, for many a bag of turf he brought poor folk in need of a fire.

During my year as Mick's right-hand man I had never known him to wear anything but the same garments and as time sped on more patches, different in colour, appeared on particularly the trousers, until very little of the original material was visible.

The number of churn cans atop the dray cart numbered ten and frequently in their midst was a smaller can which contained a sparkling white liquid. I kept wondering and wondering what sort of cow yielded such milk, so one day I questioned my hero on the matter.

"'Tis a tin cow," the old man answered not thinking. Then immediately afterwards he yelled: "Now keep your mouth shut and mind your own business or else I'll be getting myself another man."

The threat induced me to keep my tongue between my teeth in future, for another boy to have taken over Jill's reins would have really broken my heart. But curiosity still gripped me vice-like. There was something strange about that wee can.

One of the signals Jill knew best was the loud sharp whistle of the quay dockers at the riverside beneath the town bridge, where they worked at mostly coal steamers from England, Scotland and Wales.

On hearing the whistle the mare would stop dead on her step. Then the dockers, their blackened faces sweating and caps at various angles, would hasten up to the cart, mugs in hands.

Cautiously, Mick gave each docker a measure of the sparkling white liquid for a price and as they drank it I could see their eyes in the black surroundings brighten. My curiosity knew no bounds!

SAD PARTING

One Saturday morning I waited at the usual place for Mick, but he and his mare and cart didn't turn up. For hours I sat on a ditch scanning the Screen Road, but there was no sign of my hero, so in agony I walked slowly homewards throwing an occasional glance behind me, but in vain.

Weeks passed into months and when the buttermilk man didn't appear, I resigned myself to the fact that I would never see him or Jill again.

Well, Christmas time came round and one of the nice human things that happened was a kind and thoughtful schoolmaster, Harry Turbitt, organising a turkey and ham dinner and entertainment for the inmates of Coleraine workhouse and Santa was to be present with toys for the boys and girls.

I was invited along with my mandolin to play and sing. It was my first time in such an institution and I was not impressed with the whitewashed walls, bare scrubbed tables, rough wood floors and morbid lighting.

On being called to the makeshift platform I shuddered at what I saw. The members of the audience sat staring strangely at me as if they couldn't grasp the fact that a small party of outsiders had shown interest in trying to brighten their dull lives a little.

The men were dressed in baggy suits of thick black material and their hair cut to the scalp. The boys garb and heads were similar with a large hard white collar round their necks. The women and girls wore black and white striped misfitting uniforms, thick black stockings and heavy boots, which would have been more suitable for ploughmen.

I felt an upsurge of pity for those people, pin-pointed in the face of the public and submitted to a life of strict discipline and humility because they were poor, old or afflicted.

As I sang a popular ballad and played the mandolin my eyes wandered round the audience and rested on a familiar face. Heavens above! It was Mick, the buttermilk man!

When my act was over I rushed down the room and embraced the old man to the surprise of everyone. But I didn't care about the gazers around us. I had found my hero and I wasn't going to lose him again.

I sat beside the old-timer for the remainder of the concert and between acts heard his story of why he suddenly stopped coming to Killowen.. His mare Jill had succumbed to the bullet of a vet after breaking a leg. Without his faithful friend, Mick was lost, so one day John Wright and the black horse-drawn workhouse van came for him.

At the end of the concert Mick was rather crudely ordered to bed and the big matron said to me: "There's a cup of tea or lemonade for the artistes boy in my office, go and get one of them."

I didn't reply, but picked up the mandolin case, left the drab building and set off in the dark for the mill houses on the Strand Road, a distance of two miles.

Running all the way I found my mother standing on the door step talking to a Mrs McDonald. Handing the mandolin to the lady to hold, I hugged my mother and gasped breathlessly: "I'm glad to be home mammy and I'm glad to have you."

I was able to visit Mick from time to time and take him a wee bit of tobacco, the gift of humanitarian Harry Turbitt. But one day I found my hero gone!

On making enquiries I was told that Mick had died and was buried at the Ballycastle Road cemetery.

On the following Sunday afternoon my mother and I went to the cemetery and were shocked to see rows of weed-covered mounds confront us in a walled-in area hardly worthy of the respectful name cemetery.

My mother lamented, "Isn't it awful not to get rid of the scourge of poverty, even in death!"

Chapter
F I V E

MY CHRONICLE SALES HAD INCREASED TO FOUR DOZEN
EACH FRIDAY AFTERNOON ALLOWING ME ONE
shilling commission, but, to my mother's and my teacher's great
concern I was still in the third standard at school with no signs of
moving upwards. Somehow I couldn't accept the advice everyone
was giving me about the importance of a good education. A bit head-
strong I figured that selling Chronicles was much easier than
puzzling over spellings and sums.

Sister Annie, since starting work in Rogers Shirt and Collar
Factory, had become quite bossy and kept telling me off for my wee
misdemeanours and justifiably. She was now giving mother a hand
with my rearing. But deep down her love for me was strong and it
was her persistent persuasion that forced mother to let me go to a
Saturday afternoon silent film matinee. The cowboy Tom Mix and
the glamour blond Pearl White, were starring and that proved to be
a big attraction.

My going to see the special film was a personal victory, for mother's strict Presbyterianism had denied any of her children going to films of any kind. There was always the chance of seeing something bad.

The cinema was in Railway Road and it cost twopence for admission. I was taken down in the darkness to the front seat, which, in my innocence, I thought was kind of the attendant.

I was amazed at people riding horses across the big screen while printed captions beneath indicated what they were saying. Their actions were dramatised by May Bryans, our school principal's daughter, thumping a piano.

But, alas, the big film had just started when I became the victim of a multiple flea attack which, in my estimation, far surpassed the pain suffered by the cowboys and wild red 'injuns' in their screen battles.

In agony I groped my way out of the place and ran to the Northern Constitution building, a few doors away, where my mother was on her knees scrubbing.

On me explaining what had happened in the cinema all work was immediately abandoned and I was rushed home to go through the usual treatment of being stripped and put in the big tin bath with that awful-smelling disinfectant. What was about me that fleas just couldn't leave alone?

Sister Annie was present and as she boiled my clothes in suds to dispose of any of the hated creatures I may have brought home on me, mother scolded her for encouraging me to go to the flea-ridden den of iniquity.

The only part of that flea attack I found pleasing was being excused Sunday School the next morning and day school for a week. There were eleven black bites visible on my face and neck. In no way was the public at large going to get an impression that there were fleas in the Moore home - no fear!

But the pain and annoying itch of the flea bites was nothing compared to that which I later suffered with a bout of the toothache. It was terrible!

Mother was lying on top of my bed trying to console me as I wept and rubbed my jaw opposite the tormenting molar. Almost at breaking point the tired woman said: "There won't be another night like this ... you're for a dentist in the morning by hook or by crook."

In that era there were no dental services for schoolchildren. Sufferers were seen only by appointment and bills had to be paid on the spot, so my ailment was going to cause a lot of inconvenience and expense.

True to her word, mother got a two-hour pass off work to take me to a dentist and going over the Bann bridge I had the audacity to insist that my tooth was much better and that I would be able to bear it. That was the one morning I would have preferred going to school, such was the frightening name dentists had.

Mother, after trying two dentists for an immediate appointment unsuccessfully, with some reluctance finished on the doorstep of the third, who had the reputation of sometimes having to be called from a pub near his surgery to attend to patients. But he was at home on the morning of our visit and accepted me to my hidden horror!

I was seated in the hated chair nervous and shaking. After leaving a few hideous looking tools within my vision the dentist told me to open my mouth wide so that he could see inside and poke about.

After doing so he turned to my mother and said: "The tooth that's paining is a bit loose. Rather than upset your boy's system for a few days with a jag of dope I think I could have the tooth out in a jiffy without him feeling it. And the fee will be cheaper. What do you say to that?"

Without consulting the suffering figure of the experiment, mother replied: "Go ahead sir, but please be as easy as you can."

Well, the dentist went behind the chair and on putting his pliers in my mouth he hesitated, then turning to my mother again he said: "Would you take a grip of your boy's wrists and hold him down on the chair to enable me to make the withdrawal quickly and cleanly?"

Mother did what she was told and in response to a strong pull the tooth came out all right. But oh dear! I honestly thought my head was in the pliers with it.

Though in a day or two I returned to normality I still looked upon dentists as creatures to be avoided.

CHARACTERS

Killowen and its arteries of Dunlop Street, Pates Lane, Shuttle Hill and Kyles Brae, had a number of wonderful characters, whom I got to know during my Chronicle selling travels.

A namesake of mine, James Stoddard Moore, lived in one of the small Dunlop Street houses and I and other small boys sat round his fire for hours listening to his stories and they thrilled us.

He was a tramp poet self-named 'Dusty Rhodes' and he always seemed content and happy on getting his rent paid each week and a bite to eat, which was made possible by him selling printed copies of his poems around the countryside at a penny each.

His father came from Stob's Green, Edinburgh, direct to Cushendall and married Catherine, the daughter of a small farmer, Patrick Graham of Claughy. James was the only child of the union. He was born in an old corn mill in 1844.

The little education the boy received came from his father and he soon showed intelligence and a love for verse. He did much reading and eventually began to compose simple poetry.

But going into his 14th birthday he lost his parents to a fever - a sad tragic blow. It was about then that he had composed his first keepable poem 'The Penitent's Dream'.

'Twas a beautiful day in summer,
Bright flowers begemmed the valley,
Beside a bubbling fountain
In the valley were I lay.
The song birds sweetly carolled
Through the verdant woodlandalley,
When high above the tree tops
Shone the glorious God of day.

On Moore reaching the age of fifteen the call of the ocean and the desire for a roving life entered his thoughts. Leaving Cushendall for Liverpool he got a job as cabin boy on the barque 'St Dominic', sailing with a cargo to San Francisco.

In 1867, Moore enlisted in the Welsh Fusiliers and went on to serve in Malta and India. He was through the wildest part of the

Khyber Pass to Afghanistan when Lord Roberts quelled some of the hill tribes in revolt.

After fifteen years in the army the wanderer returned to his native Cushendall, and then while tramping found the homeliness of Dunlop Street nice to settle in for a period and he was well received there by the neighbours.

Careless of personal appearance, Dusty Rhodes never rallied against the hardness of a destiny that kept him on the lowest rung of the social ladder. Folk paid little attention to him as, immersed in his own thoughts, he dandered along country roads with staff in one hand and a bunch of poems in the other.

Though he could have been seen anywhere the length and breadth of Antrim and Derry, his heart lay in the beauty of the northern part of Antrim. Much of his time was spent in the Carey district. He was fondly attached to the range of blue hills there.

Ah! Who can sing the song of the moor,
With its quickening and rushing wind;
Its carving breast and endless span
Of the hills the shadows find.

The wayward genius deemed it a light task to walk the 35 miles from Coleraine to Cushendall and back and we youngsters were always waiting for him to hear more stories.

I can well remember him saying to me: "Willie son, take your chances now while you have them and give yourself a good education. It's a great thing to be able to read and understand what you are reading."

I gave a lot of thought to what the tramp poet said - more than I ever gave the counsel of my mother and teachers, but in a few days I was back in the trend of hating school as much as ever.

HOOKS AND HINGES

A Chronicle customer of mine each week was Tom Hemingway, a big ex-policeman with a thick fascinating Cork brogue. He lived at Burnside and had the nickname 'Hooks and Hinges' because of the distinct sway from side to side of his broad shoulders when walking.

In fact, all Killowen characters had nicknames bestowed upon them by a great character and 'know-all' himself, the one and only Barney Bradley. A fireside historian he knew the history of every local family off by heart and, to suit the company, could give a good or not-so-good account of them.

On Saturday mornings Hooks and Hinges never missed going to the market on the other side of the River Bann for a pig's head. And he was never alone, for costing only fourpence the head provided needy families with broth for the week by heating and stirring every day. At the weekends the tender flesh of the plump jaws was eaten and thoroughly enjoyed. Then on Monday morning the boiling procedure began all over again.

Two hundred yards down the road from the home of Hooks and Hinges lived two elderly brothers, who had long since finished from the tailoring trade to live in meagre retirement through having been regular boozers in their more active years. Appropriately, the inventive Bradley had rechristened them 'Buttons' and 'Cuttings' and that's what they were known as to the members of the local community and folk beyond.

The brothers also kept themselves alive on the pig's head diet, taking it in turn to go for the precious purchase.

One never-to-be-forgotten Saturday morning, Cuttings, who had started out on the journey to get the head with the usual good intentions, completely went astray. He had met a number of old mates who invited him into a pub for one wee half of whiskey, which turned to two, then three, then four.

After swallowing the sixth half Cuttings, who by now had neither thought for his poor brother Buttons nor the week ahead without food, dipped into his pocket for the two shilling piece that was meant for the pig's head and vital provisions. In less than two hours the silver coin, the last in the Buttons/Cuttings scanty 'kitty' had gone!

At 6pm, Cuttings, full to the neck, got an arm home from a kindly man going his way and soon he was facing an angry Buttons, an anger not aroused by his brother's drunkenness. Judging, that would have caused him envy, for he could still take a half or two himself if they came handy. It was because of the almost certainty of a hungry week ahead. Yes, a cruel lean spell faced them at a time there wasn't even a blackberry growing in the wilds.

Sunday evening came and the brothers devoured the last of last week's head. Then the famine began.

On Tuesday afternoon a depressed and hungry Cuttings picked up courage and went to Hooks and Hinges house and lied: "Due to my brother and me having the flu' on Saturday, none of us could get over to the market for the head, so today we're near deaths door with hunger ."

"Too bad." said Hooks, gesturing sympathy with his hands, "Can I help in any way?"

"Aye," replied Cuttings, a pathetic look on his face, "My brother was wondering if you could spare us the loan of your head for a boil in our own pot and we'll hand it back tomorrow? You would be saving two lives."

Hooks was thoughtful for a minute or two, then getting up from his seat he said kindly: "I'll certainly lend you my head, for I've enough broth to do me tomorrow, but I'll definitely need it back for tomorrow night to make a drop of fresh stuff for Thursday, I've friends visiting me then."

On Cuttings promising faithfully to honour that reasonable arrangement the big man went across to the pot sitting on a hob by the fire and lifting out the pig's head gave it a wipe over with a cloth, then wrapping it in a newspaper he handed the lot to Cuttings, who couldn't get out of the small house quick enough with excitement.

But, alas, Wednesday evening came and there was no sign of the head for Hooks to make a drop of fresh broth. Thursday came and passed and there was still no signs of the head, so on Friday morning an angry Hooks, now hungry himself, went down to the brothers and gave them a touch of his mind.

The big man on telling this story concluded: "When I got my pig's head back it had got so much abuse that I didn't recognise a feature on its face!"

Killowen characters and their unconscious spasms of humour were very much a part of the community. Hooks and Hinges had a close friend in the person of Joe Thom, who had the rather distinguished nickname 'The Mayor of Killowen' shortened to 'The Mayor'. And if such an office had existed there was no one more suited to fill it than Joe, for his dress comprised a black frock coat, black striped trousers, a stiff white butterfly collar with black cravat and a bowler hat.

The Mayor sold fresh milk daily, the yield of his goats, Daisy, Fawn, Brigitte, Sally, Pansy and Emma. His male goat Billy, apart from being indispensable over a wide area, was a favourite of everyone. He was seen daily following his master about the streets as a dog would and he could stand on his hind legs and beg for a carrot when someone produced one.

At the rear of The Mayor's home was a large open shed filled with hay, which was sold to jaunting car jarveys, hawkers, dealers and private folk with ponies. That service was the owner's main source of income.

But one sad day during The Mayor's absence, twenty bullocks broke out of their field, crossed the pound burn into The Mayor's yard and ate his hay.

Finding out that the bullocks belonged to a gentleman farmer, John Hughes, who lived in an imposing mansion at Hazelbank, the angry Mayor, foaming at the mouth, went along and banged on the front door of the mansion.

A maid responded and then went to inform her master that a strange noisy gentleman required his attention immediately and that was an order!

On the gentleman farmer appearing in the doorway the visiting gentleman shook his fist in front of his face and roared: "Your bullocks entered my shed in Killowen this morning and ate every bit of my hay!"

"Was it good hay my bullocks ate?" John Hughes asked, stroking his chin.

"'Twas!" The Mayor yelled. "The best meadow hay in Ireland."

"Then don't you worry yourself Mr Thom," the farmer replied smiling, "the hay won't do my bullocks any harm ... not a bit of it."

After that smooth demonstration of the phrasing of words against stormy elements the mansion door closed gently leaving The Mayor in a conundrum.

Hooks and Hinges told another tale in his inimitable manner about The Mayor of Killowen, which I think is worthy of recording for its simplicity and jest.

Hooks was coming down the street early one morning and found The Mayor standing on his front door step, miserable and his eyes swollen for the want of sleep. He had been kept awake by a swarm of moths in his home and they were destroying everything. It was agony!

Hooks told the beleaguered man to go immediately to White's the Chemists and buy himself a stock of moth balls and his troubles would soon be over.

Next morning, Hooks again found his friend standing on the door step even more distressed and exhausted than on their previous meeting. He still complained bitterly about the moth invasion of his home and of the damage the pests were doing.

"Did you not go to White's and get the moth balls?" Hooks asked.

"I did," came the raucous reply, "and I was up all night and never hit a blinkin' moth!"

CHANGE OF SCHOOL

I didn't get much of an accolade from my mother the evening I told her that I had passed from the third standard to forth, for she had already heard a whimper from inside the school that my promotion wasn't being granted through merit, but to see if I would tend to improve in a different and higher environment.

And an upcast I had to continually listen to was that Suzy's six children were beating me in every way as scholars.

If I had had any sense of pride for myself that school whimper and scholar upcast would have been humiliating. But I didn't seem to care. My constant thought was how I could escape from having to learn. Aunt Mary Jane Moore was right. I was in a rut and it didn't look like I was going to get out of it.

Then my perplexed mother got an idea into her head that a change of school might help my education problem. Through the influence of our clergyman a place was found in the forth standard of a boys school, "The Irish Society".

And a nice thing about my new seat of learning was that Harry Turbitt the humanitarian who organised the annual workhouse Christmas dinner and concert was teaching the sixth standard. That in itself gave me the incentive to reach him one day.

I had settled in the forth standard well and was paying attention to what the teacher was saying. My homework was getting top marks with sister Annie's valuable help and everything was going great until one dreadful morning.

It was an important duty of mine to go to the gasworks for a bag of coke each Wednesday morning to keep the home fire burning. I brought the fuel home on a borrowed truck and was usually at school on the dot of nine o'clock.

But this bitter cold morning I was fifteen minutes late for roll call. Unfortunately it wasn't the regular teacher, James Henry, and his cane-loving substitute wouldn't accept my going for coke excuse.

On his demand I held out my almost freezing left hand and he let me have two unmerciful wallops, which doubled me with pain. But the fanatic for making pupils scream hadn't finished with me.

"Hold out your right hand for similar treatment." he shouted, raising his cane high.

But I was having no more. Straightening myself I drew out and planted a perfect right hook on the teacher's chin, which dazed him for a few seconds. Then showing fright he threw the cane from him and running out of the classroom returned with the principal, W.P. Brown, and without hearing my side of the incident, he expelled me from the school for all time.

Chapter
SIX

I HAD ALWAYS WANTED TO FINISH WITH SCHOOL AND NOW IT HAD HAPPENED. BUT IN NO WAY WAS I pleased with myself as I walked from the red-brick building down the road to nowhere. My thoughts were with mother slaving in that mill. Her hopes of me becoming a bright scholar had ended in violence and disgrace.

How was I going to approach her with the terrible news? I just couldn't. I would bury my school bag and run away and get lost in the world. I thought again. But if I did run away it would mean the complete breaking of mother's kind heart. For a boy just the age of ten I was in an awful predicament!

I found difficulty in eating my scone lunch as I sat on a seat in the park, so the wild birds got most of it. I was broken and fit for nothing.

Then seeking a little advice or even consolation from someone I strolled along to Alex Clarke's bicycle repair shop, a favourite rendezvous of mine.

Alex was quick to notice my distressed state and when I told him what had happened he pulled a jacket over his overalls and accompanied me back to school in which I was reinstated after apologising to the teacher I hit. But I had to suffer the humiliation of demotion to the third standard. The sickening third standard again!

Mrs Smith, the only lady teacher in the Boys School, was in charge of the third standard and the lady went out of her way to help me, for there was an element of sympathy for me throughout the school because of the teacher, for whom I was expelled, not being over-popular with pupils and staff.

And so mother was spared the agonising news of my school behaviour, expulsion and demotion and showed delight at my home-work interest and progress.

Eventually I got to the fifth standard, but from there had failed a couple of times to get into Harry Turbitt's sixth standard. I was very ordinary in all subjects, especially reading and writing. It was a true fact that I would never finish my schooling to mother's expectations - never!

THINKING LOGICALLY

In November 1925, I was confined to bed through having influenza and I was more concerned about missing my Chronicle round than I was of missing school. Thankfully I had just one more year to carry a schoolbag and I would then be rid of that perpetual nuisance for all time.

While suffering from a high temperature I received a 13th birthday gift from Aunt Annie Parkhill in the form of a book, 'My Lady Of The Chimney Corner'. I quickly flung it from me. I had never read a book in my life and I wasn't going to start now. Truthfully speaking, it was doubtful if I had the ability to struggle through a book no matter how simple.

Lying in bed with nothing interesting to occupy me, gave me lots of time to think and to think more logically. I had now stretched beyond the height of my mother's shoulder and eating more than she was, with of course, her encouragement. Yet she still referred to me as wee Willie to friends. I wished that she would cut out the humiliating 'wee' and let me grow in contentment.

I thought of my destiny seeing that I wouldn't be the scholar mother had hoped for. Would I be a slave in a dusty old linen mill with ulcerated legs and a bad cough?

And I wondered and wondered why my mother prayed so much and kept thanking God. Thanking God for what? The loss of a husband and two lovely young daughters and a half-day's outing to Ballycastle from her endless bondage of toil?

I kept turning those thoughts over in my mind trying to associate mother's God with the Boys Brigade Bible Classes's God of love and mercy. There surely was a difference?

Then something within me spoke and changed the tune. "Here I was," it implied, "lying in a bed that was completely my own without the evidence of a single flea and as proof of this mounted I was made to focus on Loyal Jimmy's crude existence again and Suzy's six youngsters sleeping head to feet on a palliasse of chaff. It was then a feeling of understanding and thankfulness possessed me.

When the fever had gone and I was eating again to regain the strength I had lost, I happened to pick up Aunt Annie's birthday gift, 'My Lady Of The Chimney Corner,' just for something to look at to subdue monotony.

But on managing to read the first four pages, which were easy to follow, I found that I wanted to continue on, so beautiful and descriptive was the narrative about the author's mother and the poverty she had to endure while rearing twelve children in a hovel at Pogue's Entry, Antrim town.

I completed the reading of this book by Dr Alexander Irvine, in reasonable time and enjoyed it so much that I read it over again to my mother. She not only liked the moving story, but commended the way I read it. And my thoughtful gesture had also taken a place in her heart.

Dr Irvine's book had a powerful influence on me and it was then I was possessed of a desire to write. Silly really, for I knew I didn't have the ability, writing being my weakest subject. Certainly, I couldn't reveal my desire to be a writer to anyone at school, for it would have caused the laugh of the year! And though sister Annie had to help me construct a simple letter of thanks to Aunt Annie for her birthday gift, the literary desire still remained with me.

Dr Irvine, himself, was a great example to me. Born in 1860, the son of a cobbler, he was especially attached to his mother, who had been the mainstay in the rearing and schooling of her twelve children. In the chimney corner of her small kitchen she added to their education nightly little realising that genius was among them.

The admiration of the English-speaking world went out to Dr Irvine, not only for the ability and determination with which he rose above his humble environment, but also for his faithfulness to the high ideals he set himself. He did not devote himself to the acquisition of wealth or station, rather he gave himself to the unselfish service of man.

He passed through Yale University studying his Greek grammar in the hotel lift he operated for a living. And when he reached the heights of world fame as a lecturer, orator and author, he never forgot the needs of the class from which he sprang and maintained that any boy with the will to succeed will do so by keeping at it. That encouraging statement struck home strongly with me. It was as if I had entered a wee world of my own.

After reading and digesting 'My Lady Of The Chimney Corner' four times I started reading other books with tremendous interest. Any words in doubt I looked them up in the dictionary and got their meaning. I had taken an important step forward.

Time was marching on and I had still failed to make the sixth standard from the fifth. Lessons were now even less appealing to me. My mind was more often with the plot of the book at home with me conceiving a plan of how I would end it. And I had also my silent sessions of urging that last day at school to roll along ... please, please!

On top of my mother's disappointment that I hadn't reached the sixth standard, Harry Turbitt had told her truthfully that I was a bit lackadaisical and she had got it into her head that big word meant stupidity.

In explaining this to Suzy, the upset woman exclaimed: "Imagine saying that my wee son was stupid! Impossible! Sure didn't he read every word of 'My Lady Of The Chimney Corner' and write a nice wee letter of thanks to his Aunt Annie for sending him the book. And wasn't wee Willie a member of the school club-swinging team and a singer in the senior boys choir? There's nothing stupid about all that."

Thankfully, when the dejected woman was reeling the lackadaisical act off to our clergyman one evening his reverence interrupted to explain that the word lackadaisical meant just a little less interested not stupid, so Harry Turbitt was registered in her good book again.

One evening I had performed quite well at a school concert, not only in the front row of the senior choir, but singing two solo pieces and playing selections on my mandolin.

Afterwards the choir master, Harry Turbitt, approached my mother and congratulated her on her son's all-round musical talent. And in the course of conversation the knowledgeable gentleman explained that what her boy lacked academically he could probably make-up for in the art of music, having a natural flair for it. He should be properly taught an instrument such as piano or organ. But seeing the Moore family had neither a piano nor organ the next best instrument would be the violin. There was plenty of orchestral work for violinists.

CHRISTMAS GIFT

Christmas 1925 came and brought me a big surprise. Unfortunately one that didn't thrill me in any way. On a small table outside my bedroom sat a violin in open case with bow and a card inscribed "From Santa."

I studied the gift up and down and was instantly gripped by a feeling of disappointment. Of all the stringed instruments the violin was one I never fancied. I detested its bowing system and scratchy sound. Why hadn't mother and Annie consulted me before dipping into their meagre purses to buy such an expensive instrument?

But the thought behind the purchase was lovely and there was no way I was going to make their Christmas miserable by showing my distaste for the violin. To please them I would scrape a tune or two out of it, the board being the same fingering as the mandolin.

In less than a week I was bowing 'Derry's Walls' and 'The Sash' and mother was delighted with my progress though she continued to tell me to go lighter on the bow in case of offending the Duffins. But I was beginning to wonder if the Duffin family cared ... they seemed to be quite broad-minded.

But in my mother's absence I soon put the violin in its case and commenced reading, a subject I was now addicted to. I was also studying a tutor on simple English and was beginning to know the benefit of it. Maybe I wasn't such a dunce after all. Time would tell.

Then one day I cheekily took matters into my own hands and swapped the violin for an ancient Kentucky banjo and mother and sister Annie went frantic over what they said was the most 'sleekit' action ever performed in the Moore family history.

But when I acquainted myself with the harmonious chords of the five stringed instrument and such lovely old melodies as 'Swanee River', 'Poor old Joe' and 'Carry Me Back To Old Virginia' filtered out of my bedroom sanctuary, the pair of darlings had to break their silence and agree that the banjo was my natural instrument.

Yet, if an opportunity had arose in the midst of my intensive reading, banjo playing and singing, I would have gone gambling for pennies in a game called 'Pitch 'n Toss' and to make matters worse our venue of sin was behind Pates Lane Mission Hall. I was also guilty of smoking five cigarettes a day to become a nicotine addict. I was no longer on Sam Henry's broad straight road.

At long last I reached the age of fourteen and bade a fond farewell to school with not a very good report and though mother would have been much happier with a better one I wasn't the slightest worried. All that mattered to me was the shedding of what I considered to be years of shackles. I was now free.

In spite of my gambling and smoking habits and being no longer under the threat of a teacher's cane, I was still possessed of that strong literary interest and was now reading autobiographies, particularly of men who made the grade through their own efforts. I wanted so much to write. But the big question continually loomed. "How does one start?"

I soon got a job. I started work in Alex Clarke's bicycle repair shop at four shillings a week and the loan of a bicycle, which speeded up my Chronicle round on Friday evenings and made the job much easier.

Four shillings wasn't a lot of money, but oh how proud I was standing in front of my mother in my overalls and leaving my first unbroken pay envelope on the table with the words: "That will pay the rent mammy."

Mother smiled and her eyes moistened as she put the envelope in her purse. Then rising she embraced me with a kiss. It didn't seem to matter that I hadn't got a posh job in a solicitor's office, I was still her wee boy.

I could tell no one that I wanted to be a writer, for he or she would have instantly thought that I had gone mad! But one evening while we sipped tea I tested out mother by saying in serious tone: "I'm going to be a writer one day and I'm going to write your life story."

The dear woman laughed heartily for about a minute and I was truly vexed as I awaited her word of no confidence in me. But it didn't come. Her answer in no way implied that I hadn't the ability to write. Said she: "You would be silly son to waste your time and ink on a slave like me. There's simply nothing to write about in my moving around with a brush in a dusty old linen mill doing the same thing day in and day out. Find yourself someone of more interest."

Those modest words are indelibly recorded in my heart and I recall them from time to time to refresh the lovely memory of that evening mother gave my literary ambition a big lift.

CALAMITY

Calamity came with the closing of the linen mill. Suddenly it had given up producing the product for which it had been world famous and hundreds of people were left with no other option, but to go elsewhere in quest of a livelihood. Quite a number emigrated to countries abroad.

My mother got a job cooking for the newly formed police force, the Royal Ulster Constabulary, in their barracks at Abbey Street and though the job was cleaner, it was no less strenuous than the mill. She had to leave home at 6.15am each day and have 15 and sometimes 18 bowls of porridge and fried breakfasts on the table for 7.45am. Then came the washing of the dishes and the cooking of a three-course lunch, more dish-washing and finally tea.

I didn't feel all that happy about mother having this job, for the name police wasn't a nice one in my opinion. They had chased us a couple of times from our gambling den behind Pates Lane Mission Hall. I would have to be doubly careful in future in case I landed in a police cell under my mother's very nose. That would be a great source of embarrassment to her.

I can't blame a single soul for leading me into gambling. I found Pitch 'n Toss an intriguing game and was, so far, doing well at it financially to the despair of other boys. And selecting a horse and placing a bet on it was another regularity of mine. Seemingly, gambling was in my blood.

I still was, of course, attending Sam Henry's Bible class each Sunday afternoon. Deceiving Sam and my mother I considered to be an achievement rather than a sin. I was a liar and a hypocrite now wary of those policemen mother was feeding, for I was breaking the law with my gambling and smoking habits through being under age.

The four shillings I got for 60 hours work in the bicycle shop I was now getting for a mere 15 hours in a job I really loved. I was the 'minder' of four gun-dogs for a syndicate of seven men, who left Coleraine Diamond at 3am in two cars for a grouse shoot.

I and the dogs occupied the dickey department of the rear car and the animals, sensing the excitement ahead, kept straining on their leads. But it was a different tale on the return journey after working the front face and back and sides of a huge remote mountain. The faithful animals lay on top of each other dozing and the young minder dozed with them.

It was during those trips that I got to know several of the mountain colonies living in small thatched cabins in the midst of complete isolation. Known as peasants they had no regard for pump nor regular hours and worked their plots of land when they felt like it.

Though pitifully poor they were sharing any little they had and the shooting syndicate always reciprocated by bringing families tea and sugar, vital necessities.

The peasants seemed content as long as they had a winter's turf stacked away and a gathering of spuds in the pit. Rabbit stew was their usual diet, for, believe it or not, they weren't allowed to touch a feather of one of the game birds that flew and ran about their door steps.

I was pleased to see that they had music in their souls. Nothing afforded them more pleasure than that of attending a ceilidh round a turf fire and singing and dancing to the next morning.

One evening as I got into the dickey department of the car with the dogs, I promised the peasants that when I got older I would bring my Kentucky banjo to a ceilidh and a cheer went up.

On the long journey back to Coleraine on that occasion , I didn't doze with the dogs, but kept thinking what a great story the mountain peasants would make, particularly to city and town people, who didn't even know that such a wild sect existed. It was then, more than ever, that I wished and wished I could write.

Chapter
SEVEN

THE KILLOWEN AREA NEEDED SOMETHING HEARTENING AFTER THE GLOOM THE MILL CLOSING CAUSED AND we got it with the local Male Voice Choir sweeping the decks at Dublin Music Festival. A top London adjudicator gave the working-class songsters a record 99 marks out of 100 to leave competitors from Wales, Scotland, England and other parts of Ireland, far behind them.

On the return of the Killowen lads to Coleraine they were greeted with bands playing and bonfires blazing to the sky. I was even strumming my banjo to a crowd of jubilant folk singing, 'For They Are Jolly Good Fellows' and such was my continuing joy that after mother wrapped me in bed with lights out I waited until she and Annie were under the blankets before I got up and walked to and fro in my room with an idea in mind.

Then coming to a decision I pulled a coat over my flour-sack nightshirt, slipped downstairs to the parlour and in the bright gaslight of the outside lamp standard I commenced scribbling in my big notebook.

I was so happy and enthusiastic over our choir's success that I wanted to try and record something about it. During the celebrations I did a bit of eavesdropping to get a choir member's account of the Dublin trip, which he was giving another person, so I was quite well informed.

Getting a good start to my composition was difficult. I scribbled and scored out and scribbled and scored out, but so inspired was I that I had no intention of leaving the task.

Suddenly and thankfully I hit on an opening paragraph which pleased me. Then as I continued the words came more freely and I was enjoying my writing. At last, maybe my endless hours of reading were beginning to pay dividends?

Next morning I rewrote my composition as neatly as I could with pen and gave it a heading. 'Killowen Choir Sparkle In Dublin'. I read the finished copy over and over again and in the end I got the feeling that it might be newspaper material.

After another hour of pondering I lifted the pen and signed my name Billy Moore at the end of the brief narrative.

I didn't even have a suitable envelope to put the copy in and as I carried it carefully across the Bann Bridge to the Chronicle Office I shook like a leaf on a tree with nerves. My very first story was about to stand the test and as I now live in the late evening of life I feel that a lot depended on its success or failure whether or not I continued with my literary craze.

It seemed like a moonchange waiting on Friday afternoon for the first batch of Chronicles coming off the press. I was first in the queue of newsboys waiting for papers to sell and when I got my bagful, instead of immediately going on my round as usual I stopped in a gateway, pulled a paper from the bag and with a spittle stuck in my throat and hands that were anything but steady I started the scan for the heading, 'Killowen Choir Sparkles In Dublin.'

I hadn't too far to look, for there it was at the top right hand corner of page 3 and beneath it the name Billy Moore, in fairly large print.

Never in my young life had I ever been so excited! If I could have afforded it I would have bought every Chronicle in the bag, but soon I settled for the next best thing. As I delivered and sold my Chronicles I requested all recipients to read the choir story on page 3 and emphasised on the fact that I was the Billy Moore, who wrote it.

When I got home my mother and Annie showed similar excitement to that of my own and mother hoped with a glint in her eye and fingers crossed that the teachers of Killowen school and the Irish Society would take note of the choir story and its writer. Maybe they'll come to understand that her wee Willie is no failure.

The last thing I did that memorable night was to take a Chronicle to bed with me and mother also took one to hug.

MY FIRST DRINK

When I was fifteen a number of my stories had been printed in the Chronicle and the editor, Tom Shannon, kept encouraging me to keep on writing, particularly in the human interest vein. Harry Turbitt and other teachers of the Irish Society and Killowen Schools were surprised at my literary progress and assumed that I was getting help from a hidden hand.

However, as time went on and more of my stories appeared in the press the teachers had to accept the fact that my pen was the only one involved. And when I told them of my intensive book reading and home study they were quite astounded, but at the same time congratulated me with their best wishes for my future. That was a nice encouraging gesture, believe me.

Irish wakes were common functions with most Killowen Protestant and Catholic families in my early writing years. Folk gathered in the homes of the bereaved and after expressing sympathy started telling their best jokes and yarns and listening to those of others, the reason being to gladden hearts from their state of gloom.

I had never been to a wake, so curious, I went to one and as I listened to the jokes being spun I felt more depressed than gladdened.

My mother wasn't aware that I was present at a wake and I had no notion of telling her that I had been to one, for she didn't approve of such 'carry-ons' as she termed them.

While I was sitting there taking stock of everything a fellow came round with a tray of glasses with a red liquid in them. He beckoned on me to take one.

"What is it?" I asked.

"Light wine." he replied.

I shook my head and gestured with my hand that I didn't want it.

"Oh come on," the fellow insisted, "you've come here to share our sorrow, we would like you to share our hospitality."

Against the promises I made from childhood to my mother that I would never be caught in the web of strong drink, I lifted one of those glasses of devils liquid and sat there thinking. I could have easily disposed of it, for there was a a tin of ashes to my right, but I didn't. Instead, I kept studying the content of the large glass. It looked so innocent with its bubbles and sparkle. Then I decided to try it, but I would never take another one ... no never!

I had no difficulty sipping the wine. It was sweet like honey and trickled over the pallet smoothly. On finishing it, however, I had a little feeling of guilt and decided to leave.

But as I was going through the doorway the fellow with the tray shouted: "Have one for the road and thanks for coming."

Now did I refuse? No, no, one thousand times no! Weak and easy-led creature that I was I lifted a glass without the slightest thought for my earlier promise and swallowed the content. Oh how cunning and baffling the devil is!

Lying in bed that night under the warm stomach feeling and spell of the wine, all guilt had gone and I was thinking that my mother was something of an oddity condemning such a simple tonic like I had at the wake. It was nothing like the the rough grain whiskey that killed my father. As I have so often promised I would never touch that horrible stuff. Danger was rising in the horizon for me!

RAILWAY JOB

Seeing my father had worked to the Railway Company and Uncle James and Uncle John were still in the company's employ, I applied for a job there.

In a week I received a reply with a train ticket enclosed to come to headquarters at Belfast for an interview. That was to be my first ever visit to the city and there was no fear of me getting lost, for headquarters was attached to York Street Station, where the train from Coleraine stopped.

I was well prepared for the interview, having been tipped off by a lad who had gone through the same lot a week before.

Arriving at H.Q. I was eventually called into a large office where two gentlemen sat at a big table. Without a word of greeting they began putting a barrage of questions to me and I answered them quite smartly.

Then they directed me to a table in the corner of the office where I had to write an essay and add up and subtract a few sums, which I took some time over.

At the end of this 'back to school' ordeal came a strict medical examination by a Dr Dickey and it would have done justice to any soldier going into battle!

In the days that followed I awaited patiently on the postman bringing me news as to whether I had got the job or not. At last it came and it was heartsome. I was to start work at Portrush Railway Station on Easter Saturday, just 72 hours away!

I sang with joy and embraced my mother, Maybe now she would be able to retire from her life of slavery with my big wage coming in weekly. There was a rumour encircling that I would be picking up at least thirty shillings. Colossal!

Two old spinster aunts were so delighted with my success that they subscribed to a family fund, got up in a hurry, to provide me with a new suit of long trousers and footwear. They assumed I would have to be dressed in the best for, after all, those stiff educational and medical tests I had passed with flying colours surely justified me a job on the clerical staff if not above.

On Easter Saturday morning I was outside Portrush Railway Station a half hour before I was due to start. On leaving home a dozen well-wishers had told me how smart and manly I looked in my new suit of long trousers. And protruding from the breast pocket were two fountain pens and three pencils. I wasn't going to be caught napping with a lot of paper work for the want of tools. No fear!

At 8.55am I went to the head office and met the station master, a small portly man in a blue frock coat full of gold braid as was his cap. "You're the new boy?" he asked.

"Yes sir," I replied.

"Follow me." he said.

I obeyed and we finished in a store full of cleaning articles in sections. "Grab one of each," the station master ordered.

Puzzled and a bit down in the lip I loaded myself with a large floor brush, mop, scrubber, scraper and bucket and then was led across the station square to the 'Gents' where the station master said meaningly: "Get in there and scrub the floors, walls and bogs and I mean SCRUB THEM!"

As I entered the awful stench of those neglected quarters I gave thought to the stiff educational exam and medical test. If those were required for the cleaning of toilets, what would be required for a ticket collector's job - a Queen's University degree?

But I was to enjoy concessions. After cleaning the toilets each morning I was permitted on the platforms to help with the ever increasing holiday traffic and the tips I received, plus my wage put me in a healthy financial position.

RENAMED

My mother was now a richer woman, but common sense told her to hold on to her job in the police barrack. She wanted to be no other way but independent.

When an opportunity arose I still participated in Pitch 'n Toss and at Portrush it was easy getting a bet on a horse and now being able to afford a ten packet of cigarettes daily, my smoking had increased. The wine matter was under control. I was just having a couple of glasses of a wine called 'Red Biddy' just now and again, especially going to a concert. They made me sing and play my banjo better ... so I thought.

It was during my railway days that a cherished long-standing dream came true. I was able to purchase on the new Hire Purchase System one of the lightweight racing bicycles and already I had won a couple of junior races on it - one at Macosquin and the other at Castlerock.

Instead of using my train pass to Portrush each morning I cycled the five miles there and did the same journey back home in the evenings to become tremendously fit in spite of the smoking, which was not considered to be so harmful to health in those days.

I continued to win races with hard riding tactics and was beginning to make a name for myself in the sport. But there is one event I reflect on with some shame.

About forty competitors had entered for a triangle endurance race near to the North Antrim village of Armoy and their bicycles were not really suitable for the twelve miles task and they certainly didn't look the part of racers in their ordinary trousers with clips round the bottoms and caps turned back to front. indeed, the set-up looked more like a circus!

Those of us who had a proper strip and racing machines were handicapped 46 seconds and that was a blessing, for we got taking off in one piece.

On the first lap I was the last rider, a position of my own choice to gain wind advantage. Then going round a hairpin bend tragedy struck me a cruel blow! I got a puncture in the front wheel!

The two stewards at the hairpin bend with their flags were very sympathetic and helped me to repair the puncture. Then one said: "You can get back in the race if you want to have a go?"

I shook my head and replied: "No, the others have got too big a start on me."

Consulting his watch the steward said: "I didn't mean it that way. The others will be here in a few minutes, so if you hide behind that bush until they pass, you can slide in behind them and you're back competing for the big prize."

I stared at the proposer of this rare offer questioningly.

"If you happen to win and there are any queries, we can vouch for it that you did the three laps," the steward went on, "But I can assure you that during the crowding of the first lap you've never been missed by the boys at the starting base."

I thought of losing the half-crown entrance fee and the magnificent £1 prize and of the great honour it would be to win the race, even minus a lap and the easy-led streak within me yielded to temptation.

Well to make a long story short I won the race and there were no objections from officials, competitors nor spectators.

But I felt guilty and terribly nervous going up to receive the prize. And, who was there on the platform to present it but my partner in crime, the steward from the hairpin bend.

On handing the envelope over to me with a firm handshake the crooked official shouted to the spectators "Give this speedy merchant from Coleraine a big cheer," and they certainly did.

When I arrived back in Coleraine and opened the envelope it contained the sum of five shillings instead of a £1. The presenter and his mate had taken their big share and I couldn't say a word about it.

And on top of the scoundrel's roguery he also bestowed upon me the nickname 'Speedy' through his speedy merchant remark at the presentation ceremony. So, sadly, the 'Speedy' title is quite infamous.

Chapter EIGHT

I WAS OF THE OPINION THAT THE 'SPEEDY' TAG WAS JUST ON A TEMPORARY BASIS. BUT I WAS WRONG, FOR AS THE weeks rolled into months more and more folk were addressing me by the name. Then to put the lid on the matter, the Chronicle's chief reporter, Sam Troy, took liberty and used W. 'Speedy' Moore, under one of my stories and it stuck!

In the end I had no alternative but to accept the infamous name to identify myself. And my hope was that mother would use it and cut free from her vocabulary for all time the awful diminutive term wee Willie. Heavens above! I was now taller than her.

I had been paid off the railway job on September 30th, with the promise that I would be sent for the following summer, but my mother prayed that something else would turn up, for she couldn't bear the thought of her son cleaning stinking toilets after masses of excursionists, who bespattered everywhere except in the conveniences provided. Her wee Willie was deserving of a better future than that unhealthy drudgery - never mind the money!

That pleased me, for the busy summer job meant me missing the July 12th demonstration and that was detrimental to my orange fever, which was always at its height during July. I hadn't too long to go now until I was wearing my father's ancient sash. Roll on!

I was now getting a fee for each article published in the Chronicle and had discovered that the pen and fishing rod blend amicably. My riverside pieces were being well-received by the paper's readership.

And my Kentucky banjo was also making me some money. I was playing five nights a week in a seven-piece band which supplied the music for the famous Professor Sam Fleming's dancing classes in the upstairs department of a Coleraine building named the Knitting Factory.

The professor, a retired Army gymnast instructor, was not only Ireland's champion step dancer, but a super impresario. He once had a Minstrel Party comprised of his sons Patrick, Sammy, Willie, Hughie and daughters Letitia and Elizabeth, gifted dancers, singers and musicians. The two corner men were Killowen lads, Johnnie 'Dido' Clements and Harry 'Joker' Anderson and they were very funny swapping their wise-cracks. Indeed, each artist was of top class professional standard.

The Minstrels would go on tour throughout the Province and into Donegal from time to time and their means of transport was a two-horse drawn covered-in waggonette and it made a bonnie scene when on the move.

Each July and August the professor and his team gave morning, afternoon and evening open-air shows at Ramore Head, Portrush, and they were very popular with locals and holiday makers.

On the final curtain falling on a special afternoon show, a Scottish holiday maker, who had taken advantage of the annual Glasgow Fair excursion to Portrush came on the stage and congratulated the professor on an excellent all-round performance.

That gentleman was a coal miner named Harry MacLennon, who later rose to the top of the world as Scotland's great national comedian, Sir Harry Lauder. For years, Professor Fleming and Sir Harry corresponded and often the professor and his affable wife Brigitte were invited to cross-channel theatres where their friend was appearing. They went twice and enjoyed the wonderful reunions and Sir Harry's singing and antics on the boards. He never lost his head through fame, but was always the 'same old ninepence' using the professor's words.

LEARNING THE SAXOPHONE

Professor Fleming was a very friendly gentleman. It was he who said that I had the ability to learn the saxophone, an instrument that was putting a real backbone in dance bands. He also implied that if I was doubling on one I would be in big demand.

Impressed I went to Belfast and purchased a saxophone using all of my railway savings. I started blowing the strange, but fascinating pipe-shaped instrument and studying a tutor at the same time.

I blew and blew for several days, reckoning within myself that I was doing well. But, alas, a stiff note from a Mr W. Henry, town clerk, told me different. Part of it read.

"While the Council appreciate and encourage youth to take up music and anything of a cultural nature, at the same time we have the sanity of our rate payers to protect. We would therefore ask your cooperation in playing that instrument, whatever it is, as far away from human hearing as possible."

A bit disjointed I took my instrument along to a four acre field outside of town and practised scales there. There was no one going to make me give up what I paid dearly for.

It wasn't too long until I was able to play a few tunes on the saxophone in Professor Fleming's dance band and I was pleased to be told by the dancers that the new sound made an improvement to the outfit. I would have liked them to have told the abrupt town clerk that.

Unfortunately the Knitting Factory dancing classes had to close after Julia McLean and Jart Neill went through the floor as they swung in a set of lancers. Mercifully the couple landed in a stable below that was full of hay bales and escaped serious injury.

My next job was with Hoover Ltd in the capacity of salesman and I went to Dublin on a week's course to learn the tricks of the trade.

Picture the immensity of the scene of a city with a magnificent bay, splendid parks, massive public buildings, wide streets providing hustle and bustle, spacious and well-kept squares and elegant quays and miles and miles of built-up areas, Then sense the feelings of a green youth from the black north, who tried to find his way around.

But time is healing As it filtered through the course I found myself settling in the new environment and making lasting friendships. Things were expanding for me. I was learning.

I had every opportunity of doing well at selling cleaning machines in Coleraine as electric power had just been introduced to the town.

Knowing that Professor Fleming and his wife Brigitte lived in a long single storey house in the centre of Killowen and that they had a large fully carpeted sitting room and a grand suite I arranged to give the genial couple a demonstration of how my revolutionary machine beats, sweeps and cleans,with the hope of selling it to them.

Wide-eyed the professor and Brigitte and a number of housewives I had specially invited listened to my homely address before I attempted to clean up the dirt-spread I had put on the carpet, suite and walls and even the curtains. And I hadn't been content with that lot. I borrowed a shovel and had brought in a load of natural dirt from the street. I was going to prove the efficiency of my machine in cleaning the vile mess up.

Getting ready for the demonstration I picked up the plug and said to the professor: "Where's your socket?"

"My what?" the professor asked.

"Your electric socket." I replied.

The professor stared at me and then burst out: "My dear boy we haven't got the electric power in yet ... we still use gas."

That is an absolutely true incident, which proved my enthusiastic stupidity. But I still managed to do my demonstration very successfully by using a roll of flex attached to an electric socket about 50 yards away. And not only did I sell a machine to the professor when he had the power installed, but one to the lady who had kindly allowed me to use her electric socket.

In my mind's eye I can still see the professor vividly - his erect soldiery bearing, his smart gait, his friendly round face and those brownish grey curls his cap could never conceal.

At the age of eighty he gave his breath back to God. His cortege was one of the largest seen in Coleraine for years and I wept like a child while placing my simple floral tribute on his grave.

Today's clans in the U.S.A., Canada, England and throughout Ireland, with the blood of Professor Sam Fleming flowing in their veins should be honoured and exceptionally proud. In addition to his great performing talents and organising genius, he was a practical philanthropist. It would be impossible for me to enumerate the various charities that shared his benefactions. He was very special.

LOVE TOKEN

My mother had, at long last, managed to get herself a new black costume for Sunday worship, so she wore her dyed wedding costume to work and it continued to suit her slim figure. The wee grey mill shawl still hung on its wood peg in the corner of the kitchen. It was handy to pull over the shoulders in winter when draughts prevailed.

I was a frequent guest of mother's at afternoon tea in the barrack kitchen and several policemen were always present. They were quite complimentary towards me doubling on banjo and saxophone and playing in a much sought dance band. And they had nice things to say about my journalistic efforts in the Chronicle.

But at the same time that friendly attitude would have immediately disappeared if the same policemen had caught me playing Pitch 'n Toss, a gambling game they had been instructed to stamp out for the frustration and brawls it was causing. Really, I felt a bit guilty talking to them.

The town summons server, a slick merchant in my weighing-up, also joined us for afternoon tea in the barrack and he had always plenty to talk about in the line of meeting characters with little regard for the law. He was boring.

I was doing well, my saxophone playing having improved considerably and a column now appearing in the press fortnightly. The musical success encouraged me to form a teenage concert troupe and we were packing halls throughout the country.

I had been invited to promote a concert in Blackhill Orange Hall, between Tobermore and Draperstown and it promised to be lively and entertaining as usual.

The wireless, as radio was then known, was becoming quite popular in homes for news items and singing and music. It was announced that the B.B.C., would like to hear from good concert parties with the view to running a series of programmes on the air.

I was quick to write to the B.B.C. at Linenhall Street, Belfast, that in my opinion the 'Coleraine Teenage Entertainers' would be ideal to include in their series and that the artistes were appearing in concert at Blackhill Orange Hall at such and such a date. And I drew a map on how to get there.

In two days there was a reply from B.B.C. thanking me for my letter and informing me that two of the corporation's representatives would, possibly, be at Blackhill to listen to the artistes in the right atmosphere.

The entertainers were thrilled with the news like I was and went to great lengths to prepare. Everything must be spot on. I borrowed a suit of tails and a white bow tie for the occasion and according to the neighbours looked very professional. My mother was so emotional that tears came to her eyes as the taxi set off with the artistes, hopefully on the road to fame and mother telling the driver to be doubly careful with his precious cargo.

Arriving at the hall I judged the rows of hard wood seats hardly suitable for celebrities, so I borrowed two easy chairs from Mrs Lyle's home across the road and placed them centre front row. Then I went round turning the wicks of the paraffin lamps up to their full height.

The two gentlemen got there a few minutes past the curtain opening at eight and were ushered up to the posh seats where they settled comfortably and appreciated the warmth and courtesy shown. And I, who was doing M.C., and my fellow artistes never performed better. Without boasting we were perfection itself!

At the interval the two gentlemen were invited to the rear of the stage where strong liquid refreshments were served to them and they could certainly knock them back.

Then one of the gentlemen called me to the one side and after commending me on an all-round first-class show passed on the nastiest shock I had ever received in my years of living. Said he: "We're from the Ministry of Finance. We're here to check the entertainment tax stamps on your tickets, then we're off." Smiling, he added: "Thanks for everything."

I was speechless for a few minutes, but when a singer got the concert going again it gave me time to think. Goodness gracious! I had given the local fellow at the door a pile of compulsory entertainment stamps with the order to put one on each ticket. But, to my sorrow, I later learned that the fellow hadn't bothered with the excuse that they paid no attention to nonsense of that kind at isolated Blackhill, for it was doubtful as to whether or not the government knew of its location or existence.

In making a few inquiries I was informed that the B.B.C. and Finance worked in the same building in Belfast and that the son of a Coleraine butcher was in the high ranks of Finance, so the whole thing could have been a big joke at my expense.

I had developed into a character who continually got into predicaments and 'scrapes' which gave other folk lots of laughter and myself heartache. And, coming to my own defence, I wasn't to blame for all of them.

For instance, my mother knew nothing of the Blackhill concert mix-up and I was in no way going to worry her about it. But one afternoon I was sitting at afternoon tea in the barrack kitchen with more policemen than usual, four warders from Derry Jail and, of course, the summons server who never missed.

In the midst of a general conversation again involving my music the summons server unusually smiling broadly, handed me a piece of paper across the table with the words: "A wee love token for you."

It was a summons to appear at Maghera court and after I had read the mournful news mother plucked the paper out of my hand and on taking in the contents looked at me questioningly.

Rising from my seat I ushered the distressed woman over to the sink and explained exactly what had happened at Blackhill and she accepted it without question nor fuss.

The afternoon the summons server gave me the love token was the last time he was to enjoy Mary Edith's hospitality in the barrack kitchen, simply for the nasty manner he handled something that should have been strictly private.

My visit to Maghera court cost £17, which hardly made the Blackhill concert a profitable promotion nor one to remember with glee.

Also a frequent visitor to the police barrack was Stamper Thompson, but certainly not as a guest at Mary Edith, the cook's afternoon tea party. No fear of that!

Stamper, an instantaneous poet, was a character who periodically had a drinking binge during which he was a town nuisance and had to be put in the cell to sober. But of late he had become too difficult to handle and so finished up in Derry City's notorious jail doing a month's hard labour.

One morning he was being tried in Coleraine Court House for a grave drunk and disorderly offence and among the J.P.'s on the bench were Sir Robert Taylor, head of Coleraine Whiskey Distillery and Vance McAuley, a very big local farmer.

Studying the defendant sternly as he stood in the dock, Vance McAuley said: "Now Thompson, you are back again in disgrace. What have you got to say for yourself before we pass sentence?"

Stamper cast a glance round the Court House and then turning it upon the five members of the bench he recited.

Vance McAuley, you grow the barley,
Robert Taylor distils the malt.
Stamper Thompson drinks the whiskey,
Who then tell me is at fault?

Never in judicial history has a more logical answer been given for the defence. But, alas, the composer's reward was an extra month on bread and water for contempt.

MY FIRST SALMON

This book is in no way meant to deal with fishing, but for me to omit the catching of my first salmon would be to cheat my most cherished and exciting memory.

At seventeen I could handle the fly rod and had already landed a number of the brown speckled beauties. I went to the River Agivey's Rock Pool one mid-June morning to see if I could add to my total.

Brown trout fishing was free in that era, but a salmon and sea-trout licence for a season cost the stiff fee of thirty shillings, which was out of the range of an ordinary working man's pocket.

Half way down the big natural pool I cast under a bush and, suddenly, a gleam of silver broke the surface of the water and the tip of my rod bowed in courtesy to a fine fish. Then it jumped high in the air.

"A salmon!" I shouted aloud, "My first salmon and hooked on a trout fly!"

My heart began beating rapidly as the fish raced down the pool like a torpedo for forty yards. Then it gave an incredible display of high jumping. Failing in those vigorous bids to free itself of the hook it had another run upstream during which I kept my rod upright and a tight strain on the line. I had been well-schooled on the art of sporting a fish.

After a half-hour of battle the gallant fish rolled over on its side exhausted and my trout net just about accommodated it - a fresh-run eight pounder.

I could never adequately describe the joy and pride that filled my being that June morning as I looked down on the silver beauty. There and then I wanted to take it to Coleraine Diamond for everyone to see, but I couldn't for I didn't have a salmon licence.

Indeed, I was wondering how I would get the fish home undetected when along came the methodical Rory McElhinney, his rod over his shoulder.

On hearing of my problem he suggested that I should take the early run fish to Father Pat in the Parochial House, just down the road. He would buy it without asking any questions.

I stood staring at the old man the orange fever beginning to show its horns on top of my new-found excitement. A priest eating my lovely salmon and the 'Twelfth' only four weeks away? Not likely!

In the end I wrapped the fish in my light shower-proof coat, tied the bundle on the cross bar of my bicycle and took the precaution of travelling on the back roads and eventually I got my great prize home.

And there the silver denizen lay in state the next day to be admired by many trustworthy people, who were not allowed to leave until they heard the young angler's breathtaking story of capture.

Chapter
NINE

I WAS NOW SWINGING THE LATEST SONG HITS ON THE BANJO AND SAXOPHONE AND REPUTABLE DANCE BAND leaders were calling on me to guest with their outfits, so for a mere lad I was doing well financially. Late dances then were known as Balls and each one I played at brought me twelve shillings and sixpence, good money considering the fact that skilled ploughmen were slaving from dawn to dusk six days a week for ten shillings and a bite to eat.

Harvest Balls and Hiring Fair Balls were much longer than the city and town Balls, which were always sure to finish at the reasonable hour of 3am and seldom later than 4am.

I remember doing M.C. as well as playing my instruments at a Harvest Ball in a large barn in the district of the village of Dervock, North Antrim, and on calling the last dance at 5.15am I was accosted by a big fellow who shouted: "Hi! That"s cuttin' things short ... we don't start our work until seven."

Though just a teenager I was pleased, through my ability to promote Balls and concerts, to aid the funds of the Loyal Orange Lodge I was waiting to join. A much larger hall than the one they had was required for the ever increasing membership. In just another year I would be walking in the ranks wearing my father's sash. it would be nice if the historic lodge could have their new building by then.

When going to play at dances or perform at concerts I was still taking a couple of glasses of wine, having them in the back room of a quiet pub. And I had a secret compartment made in my saxophone case for a flat bottle of 'Red Biddy' wine, so I had added to my drinking habit by having a swig or two during dances.

And yet I was still promising mother that I would never touch the stuff. Keeping to the mildness of wine lessened any little feeling of guilt I might have had on the matter. Certainly I would never indulge in spirits. No, never!

HIRING FAIR

A few paragraphs back I mentioned Hiring Fair Balls. Those long drawn-out functions were organised in connection with the Hiring Fair, held for a day each May and November, when farmers hired boys and girls and men and women to work for a term of six months, for a most scanty wage. And if one of those hired boys and girls or men and women left a farmer's employ before time they were automatically given a six week prison sentence. It was a barbarous system.

I can recall young girls from country districts walking along the Screen Road on Coleraine Hiring Fair morning barefoot with shoes and stockings under their arms for the purpose of saving leather. They stopped at the Strand Road burn to wash their feet before pulling on the stockings and shoes and entering the crowded town with the hope of hiring to a good farmer. And there were good farmers among the not-so-good.

It is on record that the only time hired farm labourers took a stand together and came out on strike was in the large agricultural territory of North Antrim.

The farmers there with the River Bush flowing through their land had a special concession. Under the fishery owner's supervision they were allowed an annual drag of a net in one of their pools and the fish taken were gutted and put in barrels and preserved with heavy layers of salt.

Stranocum village was the place chosen for the mass protest, which was not against starvation wages, but about getting too much salmon to eat. In the days that followed, King Salmon had to take second place to humble dried ling from the nearby Island of Islay.

Perhaps I might give a better understanding of a Hiring Fair by turning to an article I once did on Dunloy's David Given. He was a tall rugged giant and when his brow wrinkled and he looked serious a stranger meeting him for the first time would have been inclined to humour him away from his aggressive mood.

But the stranger would have judged David Given wrongly, for he knew not the meaning of the word aggression. He was kind and gentle and despite the brawn and seriousness, could lift his pen and write an endearing poem on the beauty and fragrance of the rose. Such a precious gift earned for him the title, 'The Maine Valley Poet'.

At the age of thirteen David was hired to a farmer named Sammy Shaw, with whom he lived for the customary six months. And though he was up in the mornings to the crow of the rooster and out toiling in the fields he never regretted a single minute of that phase of his life.

"It taught me a lot." he claimed, "Especially in the important thing of fending for myself. Sammy Shaw was a good honest man and never once did he ask me to do something he himself wouldn't have done." With deep sincerity he added: "And his cottage was truly home to me."

But after two years far-off fields began to beckon to the boy, so at the end of term he left his employment and walked to the May Hiring Fair in Ballymoney in quest of a new master and new surroundings.

The town was packed with farm workers and David's eyes shed a wee tear as they took in boys with bundles over their shoulders, who had walked all the way from Donegal to search for a human face.

It was then a farmer approached him and asked: "Are you looking for a place, son?"

"I am." David answered.

After taking a step back and looking the big youth up and down as he would appraise a horse or cow the farmer asked: "Have you got your character handy?" (meaning a reference).

"No, but I can get it within an hour, so I'll meet you here then and take the shilling." A shilling, or rather the King's head on it, was the binding link between master and servant.

The farmer agreed and so the pair met in an hour. "You got your character?" the farmer asked holding out a tempting shilling.

"No, I got your's instead and I'm not coming with you." replied the youth spiritedly.

In a couple of days a broken David picked up courage and returned to Sammy Shaw, who welcomed him with open arms. This is a poem on that early venture which was found in the poet's collection years later.

On the road from Rasharkin,
That leads o'er the mountain,
And down through Duneaney
    onward to the Maine,
There stands a wee cottage by
    the side of the fountain,
It brings back sweet memories
    again and again
'Tis forty long years since
    lonely I cherished
The glow of the fire, neath a roof
    thatched with straw
For friends I had few and oft
    would have perished
Had it not been for the kindness
    of brave Sammy Shaw.

I being light-hearted and youth
　　was adorning
I craved for adventure and in
　　strange parts to roam,
But fate brought me back in the
　　grey of the morning
To the cottage on the brae,
I always called home.

DRINK PROBLEMS

Killowen had its big share of drink problems. Most of the dock workers came from there and following the unloading and loading of ships they hastened to a nearby pub for a pint to wash the coal dust or flour dust or potato dust from their throats.

But, sadly, that first pint led to another and another, then came the halfs of whiskey, so that at the end of the session the mugs had slaved hard all day for the benefit of the publican rather than for their wives and children back home.

Suzy's docker husband Hugh was still a victim of this weakness of drinking his wages or most of them and like my mother the wee woman hated drink. She was now in a large tin shed on her knees from 8am to 6pm grading potatoes for shipping.

After the closing of the mill she and a number of other women had no alternative but to take this job and their hands were frozen and twisted in winter without heat and in summer were almost roasted alive. They were known locally as "pratty graders."

To keep old friendships made in the mill over the years intact, my mother often invited Suzy and a number of other 'pratty graders' for a cup of tea and a chat round the fire.

I was in our kitchen one evening when the women arrived and was about to leave when Suzy pushed me back into my chair and said: "We would like you to join us ... you may get something to write about."

Ater tea Suzy told the story of poor helpless cattle drover, Harry, who lived two doors above her in Dunlop Street and whom she never saw hungry for a drop of broth when she made a pot.

Harry was a quiet innocent being in sobriety, but on getting paid for delivering cattle or sheep from a dealer or farmer, he made for a pub near his home and got drunk. On leaving the pub he had a quite unbelievable habit of throwing whatever money he had left up in the air. And a few old-fashioned boys were always around to pick the coins up.

But one night a drunk Harry made his way home from the pub without having thrown any money away. As he was going in the doorway the boys following him shouted: "No money the night Harry?"

It was then the drunk turned and putting his hand in his pocket tossed his money to them .. every ha'penny of it.

That was to be poor misguided Harry's last handout, for some hours later he choked on his vomit and was found dead in the morning.

On the late afternoon of the fatality the black horse-drawn workhouse van came and put the unsightly corpse in a black box which was put in a flowerless paupers patch at Ballycastle Road.

While Suzy told that pathetic story she never lifted her eyes off me. Surely she must realise that that type of writing drama was out of my depth? Then while in bed that night I had another inkling as to why I had been the wee woman's main target earlier. Did she know about my brief drinking spells? If so, would she tell her friend Mary Edith about them? The constant worry denied me of any sleep and dawn came as a relief.

STRICT WARNING

Next day I continued to worry in case Suzy had communicated anything to mother about my drinking, but on coming home from work that evening the boss of our home was in a good mood, indicating that all was well and that my terrible thoughts about Suzy amounted to nothing but silly imagining.

What better way could I have celebrated the joyous outcome, but by having a treat from the secret bottle in my saxophone case, That night I required no rocking to sleep, believe me.

However, I happened to meet Suzy in Killowen Street the following Sunday morning going to the Parish Church with her six children and they were well grown now.

What a gallant wee woman this was - six days a week in rags working in an old pratty shed. Now here she was, dressed like a real lady and on her way to worship, a golden example to other Killowen folk less church conscious and there were many of them.

Stopping me she said: "You may think that what I'm going to speak to you about is none of my business, but I feel that my respect and love for your mother, Mary Edith, makes it very much my business, for I never want to see her hurt in any way."

Suzy paused for a moment to make sure none of her children were within hearing distance then she continued: "Your rearing has been heavenly compared to that of other youngsters, including my own. You always had a clean comfortable bed to sleep in and you never had to go to school barefoot. You didn't get that comfortable bed, good clothes and footwear without your mother having to work her fingers to the bone and suffer the continuous agony of ulcerated legs and fibre dust in an old mill."

The wee woman, now boiling over, took three steps towards me and went on: "We all know that you've your mother's love and trust. And we also know that you're betraying that love and trust behind her back by drinking, of all gut-rots, that cursed 'Red Biddy' which is causing human destruction! I see it around me every day. I even see it in my own home."

Then Suzy's tone softened as she appealed: "For the sake of the lovely gentle woman who bore you son and your own entire future, please give up this drinking at once." Smiling she added, "My family and I will be praying for you in church."

I was completely taken aback by Suzy's talk and didn't have the words within me to reply. How the heck did she find out about my drinking? And how did she get to know that I was indulging in 'Red Biddy'? Some sneak was squealing on me, so I would have to stop going into that pub. One consolation was, Suzy hadn't told mother of my drinking and neither had she threatened to do so.

Then I began thinking on a personal trend at the same time giving myself a bit of sympathy. What was I supposed to do with my own life to please other folk? Put myself into seclusion and grow up a moaning miserable old man? Were they not going to allow me the freedom to oust my youthful vigour and enthusiasm? Was I to be denied a simple glass of wine, merely a natural fruit juice, because of my mother's and Suzy's fears that it would lead me to the fires of hell? They were mistrustful, unsociable and unfair!

Chapter
TEN

AT LONG LAST MY EIGHTEENTH BIRTHDAY CAME AND I
HAD RECEIVED QUITE A NUMBER OF GREETINGS CARDS
from friends. For the past week our oven pot had been in constant
use with mother making wee scones and currant and raisin cakes.
The kind thoughtful woman had arranged a party in our home and
when the guests arrived they included Suzy and family, so I had to
be on my best behaviour.

I had stopped going into the pub, but hadn't stopped drinking. I
was now relying on the portable bar in my saxophone case for
stimulants and was stocking it by cycling to the back entrance of a
pub in Ballymoney to make my purchases and where, I hoped, there
were no sneaks to spy on me.

At the party I played the banjo and, seemingly, everyone was
pleased. To me, however, it was boring though I had to look happy
for the sake of the organiser. I longed for a mouthful of 'Red Biddy'
to put life in me, but, of course, that was an impossibility with so
many strong-smelling nostrils present. I was properly cornered!

Getting around town and countryside searching for stories at the age of eighteen, I had to adapt the title 'Speedy' to identify myself. Everyone I met addressed me by that name with, of course, the exception of my mother. Though I was now looking down on her she still called me wee Willie and I had given up hope of her ever calling me anything else.

In the days that came the one great moment I looked forward to was the 'ride on the big Billy goat'. That was an old-time saying expressed to young men about to be initiated in the Loyal Orange Institution and it caused them much excitement. I could hardly sleep during the nights approaching my 'ride'. Each one brought the glorious day closer, the glorious day I would wear the sash of my loyal forebears in public.

I was now a permanent fixture of a well-known and popular dance band named 'The Night Hawks'. Mother didn't like the far travel and early morning home-comings dance work involved and would have much preferred me concentrating on full-time writing. But though I was keenly interested in journalism, I couldn't leave the music scene. It was a big part of my life.

The day I had waited long for fell on a Monday. That evening I was to be made a loyal son of William the Third. The night before in bed had been one of exciting restlessness and now only hours remained to the start of the great ceremony and it was nerves and all go as I prepared.

I had a nice neat haircut, a body rub down in the big tin bath and clean clothes from the skin out. I wore a snow-white shirt and a red, white and blue tie. My suit had been newly pressed and, last, but by no means least, my breast pocket accommodated a handkerchief with His Glorious Majesty on his big white stallion embroidered on it. Was it any wonder my mother hugged and kissed me and acclaimed me the perfect orange and purple candidate?

That memorable night of nights I came home from the Orange Hall, following my installation, walking on air. I was now a fully-fledged orange hero truly intoxicated with the dew of the Boyne and now patiently awaiting the Twelfth to give the famous family sash its first outing in years. What a day that was going to be with history repeating itself in a lovely way. No surrender!

But one month later I was strolling across the Bann Bridge when I met a firm brother of the loyal movement, who gave me a terrible shock. Said he: "The head ones in the lodge are not too keen on you playing at dances in Catholic Halls. You played at one last week and they continue to keep an eye on you."

It was only natural for me to get myself into a state of nerves over this awful predicament. The following night I was booked to play at a dance in the Catholic Hall the fellow had mentioned. What was I to do? The band, with a full Protestant membership, needed me and I needed the money.

I went on and played at the dance keeping my head well down, but in vain, for my presence was spotted and so I was expelled from the lodge, not for nine years nor nineteen years nor fifty nine years, but for a mammoth ninety nine years!

Sad and dejected I had to put the family sash back in the bandbox with a lot of moth balls, for July the Twelfth, 2029, is going to be a long time rolling around.

MOUNTAIN VISIT

Readers will recall me writing about being a dog minder at the age of twelve, for a shooting syndicate that shot grouse among a mountain colony of peasants who lived in small thatched cabins and who had music in their souls.

I had promised to bring my mandolin and play for them, but never managed to find transport. And though a number of years had passed since then I hadn't forgotten and in addition to giving them a musical evening I had a burning desire to write an article on their humble way of living.

A visit to there was made possible when I had the good fortune to meet a very gifted piano accordionist answering to the name of Leo Culkin. He and I played a lot together and our specialities were Irish jigs and reels and lovely old-time Irish waltz tunes. Ideal stuff for my mountain friends.

Leo had a grocery establishment and a van, so good sport that he was he decided to come with me and not only did he bring his accordion, but a load of eats for our hosts, who hadn't the slightest idea we were coming.

Most of the peasants remembered the boy dog minder and gave us a warm welcome. And when they heard we had instruments in the van and were staying for the night the large cabin of Dunger and Rosie Donnelly, was taken over and after the bed, table, dresser, cradle, chairs and even the big pot were left outside, the dancing commenced.

As couples swung in the 'Haymakers Jig,' sparks could be seen flying out of the stones their fast-moving boots dug up from the earthen floor. It was a powerful night, the like of which was never seen beyond the big brae before.

At a deserving break for the musicians, bowls were handed to everyone present and a big jug of poteen did its round providing fairly large measures. I was wise enough to stop any going into my bowl. Of course, Leo and I had a bottle of wine of our own to keep our spirits in tune with the dancers.

Before the last dance was called, breakfast was served and it comprised rabbit legs and breasts, chicken, grouse and hedgehogs, all baked in clay and roasted in the big turf fire. Before turning your nose up at such a meal, let me explain that it was healthy digestible delicious food.

Later, I wrote an article in on my mountain visit naming it 'The Lost People' and it caused quite some interest. My mother read it over and over and commended it to the policemen as we sat having tea in the barrack kitchen on the afternoon it was published.

Later, the head-constable appeared in our midst with a paper in his hand and made a favourable reference to the two-column article. That head-constable was the father of my musical partner, Leo Culkin.

SHAMED

As I have already stated I considered myself the target of 'clipe-clashers', an old Irish tag for those despicable beings who stoop to spy on other folk and tell tales about them. Already they had stopped me going into that old out-of-the-way pub for a wee gargle and a bit of innocent crack and their underhand squealing had got me expelled from the Orange Order.

But in spite of those setbacks I was now feeling an element of freedom and independence. I had my own wee secret portable pub in my saxophone case and with a ninety-nine years wait in front of me before I wore the family sash, my former orange enthusiasm had greatly lessened. I could play my instruments wherever I want now without having to keep my head down.

One unforgettable Friday evening I was asked to play my banjo at a youth party and had arrived on time. I had also taken my saxophone along, not to play, but for the convenience of the flat bottle of 'Red Biddy' concealed within. A couple of mouthfuls during the party would put jizz into my fingers. Even at that early stage of my life I could never picture a session of entertaining without a drop of the stuff.

The boys and girls present were bright and lively and took part in every game called. Then at an interval one of the organisers brought me refreshment which looked like a tumbler of mineral.

"What is it?" I asked.

"Lemon soda laced with a little gin to put a body in it," came the reply, "you need a tonic to keep going on your own."

"I don't touch spirits," I replied.

"Spirits wouldn't be allowed at this party," the fellow explained, "What you've been offered with the committee's best wishes and appreciation is a diluted beverage." Shrugging his shoulders he said, "I'll leave it on this chair beside you and you can either take it or leave it."

As I played for another game I kept the tumbler in the corner of my eye. And when I finished playing I sat staring at the drink still fuzzing with an inviting merriness. But I had been warned so often to beware. There was a dog in front of me with a friendly wagging tail, yet it could show vicious snarling teeth. I didn't know which to believe.

But after the next game my weakness betrayed me again and I went for the friendly wagging tail. Lifting the glass I sipped and was surprised at how pleasant and refreshing the content was.

Draining the tumbler, I left it back on the chair reckoning that another couple of those diluted beverages would save me the trouble of opening my saxophone case for the 'Red Biddy'. The one I had just swallowed certainly had a kick. Hopefully the kind gentleman would attend to me again.

And true to my wishes he did keep replenishing my glass and I enjoyed every sip. It wasn't as raw as 'Red Biddy', but then it would be much more expensive.

At the end of the party at midnight I felt a bit staggery. There were no worries though. Mother and Annie would be in bed as usual. I would slip indoors with my own key and get to bed and that was that.

But I hadn't really finished with the diluted beverages yet. As I walked out of the hall with my instruments the liberal organiser, who had looked after me so well shouted, "The committee members are having a wee dram for the last ... come and join us."

I stopped on my step and stood in silence for a moment. I knew I had enough drink in me for one night, but couldn't bear being unsociable, so I went over to the gathering and accepted another drink.

This time, however, I could taste more gin than lemon soda. Nevertheless I swallowed it and was foolish enough to allow my glass to be filled again. I don't think there was ever a person born with less will-power than me. Confronted with temptation such as this I just couldn't say no and maybe didn't want to say no.

I finished the second drink, left the empty glass on the table, thanked the five gentlemen for their warmth and hospitality and walked towards the instrument cases at the door. But I never got there. Half-way, something exploded within me and I dropped on the floor totally unconscious.

Four of the committee men took it upon themselves to take me the short distance to my home and kept knocking on the door until my mother responded. On seeing my lifeless form carried into the kitchen she went into hysterics and Annie, in tears, had to direct the gentlemen upstairs where they laid me on my bed still completely out for the count!

At last one of the gentlemen managed to make my mother understand that I hadn't been knocked down by a motor car, but had taken a wee drink over the half dozen. I would soon sleep it off. How sad! What a detrimental statement to make to a drink-hating mother, who was of the opinion that her son was a temperance puritan.

When mother went upstairs and saw me lying there not able to speak to her and my face as white as a ghost, she insisted that she wanted a doctor immediately and one of the gentlemen said he would send a doctor friend of his along, so he and his colleagues got away at last from the terrible drunken scene, which really, they had created.

The doctor arrived and after removing my tie and opening my shirt collar and pulling off my shoes, he adjusted my senseless body to the position of belly down. Then turning to my anxious mother said, "Your son's suffering from a hangover."

Mother, noticeably confused asked, "What's a hangover doctor?"

"You're son has had too much to drink, but he will be all right in a day or two ... just let him sleep it off." the doctor said.

The doctor's night visit cost my mother her entire savings, but that was the least of her worries. She had certainly suffered because of her husband's persistent drinking, but he was never carried home in the deplorable stupid state her son was. And she never suspected that he ever touched the devil's liquid as his promises not to had been so sincere. Please God never let it happen again.

And my mother's excellent attendance record at the police barrack had been severed by my awful behaviour. In no way could she leave me lying at home senseless to the world. That resulted in another cook being engaged to take her place for a couple of days.

I became semiconscious the next day with a steam hammer beating at my head. I was shaking all over with sweat pouring out of me in streams. The horrible treacherous Madam Alcohol was taking her toll.

An unsightly object stretched out on the bed I was like a robot waiting to be switched on. I neither knew who I was nor where I was.

At last the events of the night before revealed themselves to me and it was then I arrived at the bitter truth. I was in my own bedroom but couldn't remember how I got there. Then to my horror I discovered that the sour contents of my stomach, in my senselessness, had gushed through every escape route of my fully clothed body. My throat and nose were clogged with the filth, but it didn't hinder my nostrils from taking in the unbearable stench that filled the room.

I tried to assess what had happened. I remembered taking the last drink and passing into oblivion. Then I shuddered and the shakes and sweats increased as I realised that I must have been brought home by those fellows and handed to mother in a terrible drunken state.

In the name of decency had those fellows no thought for a mother's sensitive feelings, bringing me home to her at that hour of the morning and disturbing sister Annie as well. Why didn't they let me sleep it off in the hall?

As I lay in agony and filth I was somehow committed to reflect on my mother's past life and my tears flowed freely. I could see her come home from the mill and bath her swollen feet and ulcerated legs; I could see her finish in the mill at midday on Saturdays and hobble across to the Northern Constitution building and on her knees scrub it out from top to bottom so that Etta, Jeannie, Annie and me should have toys at Christmas; I could see her sitting at the bedsides of her dying daughters, giving them her love until her eyes closed with sheer exhaustion from endless toil and I could see her deep concern and tears for me when the Downhill baronet whipped my frail body, neck and legs.

And the only form of reward the brave woman ever asked off me was that I grew up to be a decent God-fearing citizen. Now my reciprocation for her lifelong love and sacrifices was to be handed to her stupid and filthy through drink - the fiend she dreaded most!

Eventually mother entered the room and her countenance gave evidence of her grief. She didn't shout and rave, but looked at me and asked: "What do you think of yourself today?"

"I'm truly sorry mammy for this heartbreak I've caused you." I mumbled weeping.

Then mother said: "I would like those stinking clothes off you and the bed sheets, pillow and blanket till I get them boiled and washed. And I have the disinfectant ready to scrub out this room, which I will also have to fumigate with sulphur. I never want the smell of cursed drink in my clean home. Never!"

Then when mother was leaving the room she wheeled round and said: "I have a clean set of clothes for you airing in front of the fire and the big tin bath is ready in the scullery for your filthy body."

Raising myself on my right elbow I found voice to say: "I will never drink again mammy ... I just couldn't mammy."

Chapter
ELEVEN

IN THE DAYS FOLLOWING THAT HORRIBLE DRUNKEN
LETDOWN I WAS SICK AND SHAKY AND VERY QUIET
when at home. And my mother and sister Annie were also quiet.
Like myself they just couldn't get over what had happened and I
was hopelessly lost in trying to find a way seeking their forgiveness.
That seemed utterly impossible after the trust mother had in my
promises, some of them made over the open Bible.

It was mother herself who ended the silence between us. Putting
her hand on my shoulder one evening after tea she said: "I have
been thinking things over and maybe what happened on Saturday
morning was God-sent to show you how ruthless cursed drink can
be in causing suffering and humiliation."

I agreed with a nod of my head and really meant it, for distasteful
symptoms of the hangover still remained, especially those frightening spasms of shaking. Just then I was fully intent in spending the
rest of my life a temperance advocate. I had learned my lesson the
hard way. I definitely had!

But in the midst of my sickness and temperance plans had I gone upstairs to my saxophone case and flung away the flat bottle of 'Red Biddy'? No, I hadn't.

My thoughts of permanent sobriety changed in a hurry. In less than two weeks I was back on the 'Red Biddy' and, rather audaciously, had gone a stage further by having a hefty afternoon slug at home in mother's and Annie's absence. The promise I had made to mother in the bedroom was as worthless as the others. I figured that a drop of wine was harmless. Didn't French, Italian and Spanish folk of all ages drink it by the gallon? Certainly I would never touch the hard stuff again to hurt my mother in any way. There was no fear of that.

What a hypocritical theme! As I now dwell in the late evening of life and look back on those years of deceiving the woman who thought the sun rose and set on me, the woman who bore me, I feel utterly ashamed. Thankfully, that was only part of my make-up. I had a keen sense of humour and got on well with people as my human-interest writings over the years show.

My fishing trips to Aghadowey, not only gave me good bags of trout, but a lovely wife. Cupid had introduced me to Margaret Milliken and soon we got married and went to live in her grandmother's cottage, which was located in the midst of an angler's paradise - the big Agivey, the wee Agivey and Rhee. Some days I had one of those rivers all to myself.

Granny Milliken's cottage was equipped with one of those sensational wireless sets and in the evenings farm worker friends of the family would join us around the big fire and there in the sombre light of a paraffin lamp we would listen in wonder to people speak and sing in London.

I remember a fireside philosopher say after we had stood for the National Anthem: "They'll be attachin' movin' pictures to them things next." We laughed heartily at his remark ... we thought he was mad!

Aghadowey, the largest rural district in Ireland, had a very prosperous linen industry in the first quarter of the last century, which employed hundreds of folk, particularly in the cottage spinning capacity.

But, alas, when I went to live there the once vast concern was on its last legs and like the Coleraine linen mill eventually closed down for all time, leaving the unemployed with two options - local agriculture or immigration.

INTERESTING HISTORY

I soon became a student of Aghadowey history and had a number of articles published on my research. I'm prompted to record a couple of points for posterity.

The Reverend James MacGregor was ordained as minister of Aghadowey Presbyterian Church in 1701. But due to strict penal laws he led a colony of his flock to the 'new world' in which there were opportunities for men of character and with industrious ideas.

Mr MacGregor's fleet consisted of five small ships and they set sail from Coleraine Harbour carrying 700 souls, the oldest of them being in his 96th year. He was a Ballymoney man named John Young and he lived until he was 107.

The colony landed at Boston on August 4th, 1718. Eventually, a contingent of them made their way to Nutfield and greatly helped with the building of the City of Londonderry.

Mr Green, an American historian, addressing the American Antiquarian Society, at Boston, on April 25th, 1895, had this to say about MacGregor's colonists: "They were notably men of practised sagacity and common sense. They were self-reliant and persistent, brave and fond of adventure. They were plain, industrious and frugal. They were frank even to the point of rudeness sometimes. Their sedateness was relieved by a sense of humour. They had a passion for education and religion and very strict in their morality. They were really the schoolmasters of all the leaders of the revolution, who lived south of the city of New York. They demanded religious liberty for themselves, but they allowed it to others."

IN THE ARMY

In 1939 I was doing well with my writing for the press, but had forgotten about mother's Bible teachings and what I had learned

under the instruction of Sam Henry at the Boys Brigade Bible class.
I no longer attended church nor prayed, nor believed in God.
Indeed, I was a confirmed agnostic and would have argued against
scriptural quotes.

My mother wasn't fully aware of this stand I had taken since
leaving home and her parental rule, but had suspicions that my life
was not being lived as she had wished. She didn't chastise me
severely any more, for she had allocated me a small room of her
new home at Long Commons, Coleraine, to do my writing for the
press and didn't want to annoy me in any way in case I stopped
coming.

The brave woman had retired from work after an unblemished
55 years and was now living on an old age pension. She was
remarkably active and here I must praise my sister Annie, who had
decided to stay with mother and take care of her should any form of
health decline set in. What a lovely thoughtful gesture from a girl
who could have had a happy marriage with possibly a family.

Doing my writing in the mornings I was always reasonably
sober when going into mother's and if I had to visit her with drink
taken I stood a distance from her sucking a peppermint lozenger to
camouflage any smell.

But I was fooling no one for mother could read the curse of
alcohol in my eyes and detect its redish purplish flush on the cheeks.
Sadly she had become an expert of that particular diagnosis from
the early days of her marriage and was very much aware of the
disastrous complications that can arise from it. That was the chief
reason for her concern about my drinking. And it was no longer
wine I was indulging in, but whiskey, the drink that killed my
father.

Progress enabled me to buy a typewriter and a motor car, both
second-hand, but quite capable of doing what I wanted of them. I
could now batter out the articles from my rough notes and the
resultant copy for the editor and linotype men was easier to read
and much more professional than the usual scrawl.

The use of the motor car certainly broadened my writing, fishing
and shooting horizons. I was now frequently visiting 'the lost
people' in their wild mountain country and getting a 'shot' at the
grouse through the courtesy of Finbar, the 17-year-old nephew of

The Moore family photographed in the Summer of 1913. Wee Willie (the author) is flanked by his devoted sisters Etta (centre), Jeannie (seated) and Annie.

The author at the age of six. A year later he was selling Coleraine Chronicles.

Stephen Brown's painting of the author's mother, Mary Edith, in the linen mill where she worked.

Dunlop Street, where Suzy and family existed.

The tramp poet, 'Dusty Rhodes' whose verse and logic were an education to the author.

A thatched section of Killowen Street, where the author grew up.

The author was much happier in the school club swinging team than he was attending lessons.

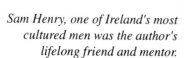

Sam Henry, one of Ireland's most cultured men was the author's lifelong friend and mentor.

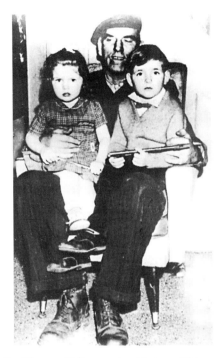

David Given, the Mourne Valley poet, with two of his grandchildren.

The author as a member of one of Ireland's first Show Bands 'The Night Hawks'. Pictured left he is the only surviving member.

The author at the age of thirty.

The author, when in the RAF during the war, is seated on the tail of a Nazi bombing plane which a Spitfire had just shot down in France.

The wonderful staff of Hopefield Hospital, Portrush, where the author regained health and found lasting peace.

Victor Hutchinson at the controls of the aircraft and the author just before taking off on a flight to Shetland.

Pilot Michael Kirk, colleague of the author, who was killed when his plane crashed near his farm at Ballymena.

Dunger and Rosie Donnelly, whose parents and two sisters had died in a fire. His abode was a timber shed attached to the gable end of the Donnelly cabin and he invited me to stay there for any span of time I desired. It was just a matter of lifting the latch and walking in. Finbar was master of the shot gun and his splendid double barrel twelve-bore type had been presented to him when he agreed to patrol and protect the game mountain territory of an Omagh syndicate and he had thinned down the fir and feathered predators considerably and scared off a few human as well.

Driving the car I had to watch my drinking, yet the best place to find a good character was in a pub. I visited them in all parts of country districts and when introduced to a suitable subject I would buy him a pint and a whiskey while I had a mild beer. He always talked much better well lubricated.

But on arriving back at the Aghadowey cottage I always made up for my lack of gargles on duty by having three or four whiskeys. Then to end the evening on a cheery note I would walk to one of the four pubs available, for a few pints of beer and a bit of good crack. To my young peaceful non-complaining wife, her mother-in-law's sordid drink history was beginning to repeat itself.

In the summer of 1939 I was guesting seven nights a week with a band named 'Candy and his Commanders' in a large Portrush tourist hotel and did a comedy spot of entertaining in the hotel cabaret.

IN THE ARMY

I was also a member of the Sixth Light Territorial Battery, Royal Artillery, booked to go on a fortnight's training stunt to Morecombe, England, at the end of September. But the war happened to break out on September 3rd and spoiled for us what we thought was going to be a nice holiday by the sea.

We automatically became regular gunners in the Army and were based at home awaiting an overseas posting to a war zone. When we received news that the battery was to leave Coleraine on a certain date I motored to the mountain for a shot and a session of music and to say farewell to my friends there for an indefinite period.

Dunger and Rosie Donnelly, with a smile, again agreed to a lot of furniture moving so that their cabin be used for a ceilidh and I played the banjo for singing and dancing until the morning and never seemed to tire, so enjoyable was the function.

After a couple of hours sleep in Finbar's shack I got in the car to leave for home a bit sad. The big youth and I had already embraced and said farewell. But suddenly he opened the passenger front door of the car and jumped in, solemn faced. "I'll leave you to the foot of the mountain." he said.

There was silence for half-way, then Finbar resumed talking quietly, yet seriously. "I've a notion of giving the birds and vermin a rest and trying my aim on a wheen of 'Hitlerities' for a change."

"You're thinking of joining the army?" I asked.

My friend nodded.

"Living in Northern Ireland, you're not compelled to join. There is no conscription here." I explained.

But Finbar just shrugged and mumbled: "I've my mind made up ... I'm going if they take me."

They certainly did take the fine specimen of manhood, for I had a letter addressed to the Chronicle Office, Coleraine, five days later with information that he was in uniform and had started training. What had poor Finbar to fight for? Poverty and starvation?

When the Sixth Battery was about to depart from Ulster's shore I reckoned that I would be better to slip away without visiting mother at Long Commons and upsetting her emotions. She didn't take partings easy and certainly wouldn't this one involving her only son going to the dangers of war. On arriving at my destination I would write her a long letter explaining why, thoughtfully, I hadn't called. That would prove my strong affection.

And, what's more, I couldn't leave my dear native town without showing true patriotism and having a few drinks for the long road to dear knows where. I had promised my territorial comrades to be in the Station Bar a couple of hours before train departure to lead a sing-along of popular songs on the banjo, especially 'Now Is The Hour When We Must Say Goodbye'. How appropriate.

But my mother, who was informed of the time the military train was pulling out of Coleraine Station by the mother of a territorial, was taking no chances of not seeing wee Willie leave, so when I hadn't turned up at a certain time to give her that final hug and kiss, she quickly accepted a lift to the railway station in a neighbour's car.

At last my anxious mother, dressed in her Sabbath best, found my whereabouts in the middle section of the train and called me to the window, where I stuttered out my weak excuse for not calling to see her.

"I can quite understand," she replied, then added: "I have a special reason for seeing you."

Dipping deep down in her faded handbag she produced a small Bible and there were tears in her eyes as she handed it to me.

"Son," she sobbed, "I want you to read a portion of that wee book every day and accept it into your heart and you'll never go wrong."

"I will mammy, I will." I promised as I kissed and hugged her. Then the moving of the train parted us.

The battery was comprised of three troops and the one I served in was based at the town of Grangemouth, Scotland, quite a precarious posting, for our anti-aircraft guns were entrusted to protect the Scottish Oils, a mass of giant petrol tanks. Never mind a German bomb, a live cigarette end dropped by a careless gunner would have set the lot alight.

I was fortunate to be selected as batman to the troop commander, Lieutenant Brian Clark, a director of William Clark & Sons, Upperlands, world famous producers of Irish linen. Apart from rank we had something in common, he was a shooting man and a top-class shot.

It's quite unforgettable the day Brian was invited to take part in a pheasant shoot on the Calandar House estate, Falkirk, which was teeming with the colourful birds. I was taken along as my officer's gun loader. He had a pair with him, so I had the occasional shot and we missed few of the easy targets.

It being a cold day the gesture of Game keepers Smith and Bennet in leading the shooting party to the Saddle Room for a drop of vintage Scotch was very fitting.

Then Brian and I had a pleasant surprise. The housekeeper of Calandar House, Miss Haddow, invited us indoors for coffee and to look at the interior, explaining that the owners, the Hon Mr and Mrs Forbes, were away on war duty.

We gratefully accepted the kind invitation and on removing our wellingtons entered the imposing building in which Kings and Queens, over the years, have stayed.

Following coffee and an informative chat with Miss Haddow, the charming lady directed us around and we were intrigued at the well-preserved relics. The first room we were shown was once occupied by Bonnie Prince Charlie, whose personal letters in frames were displayed on the walls.

Miss Haddow then took us through a long richly carpeted corridor and there was the magnificent staircase, used by Oliver Cromwell, when he captured the house and made it his home.

We were directed to other rooms complete with beds, clothes and laced pillows. A plaque had this inscription. "These beds were slept in by Mary Queen of Scots and her ladies."

A brass plate on the ground floor informed us that the Hon Mrs Forbes was a direct descendant of Oliver Cromwell and on us leaving the mansion, Miss Haddow, who herself was aristocracy, further explained that Queen Victoria had also stayed in the mansion for quite some time.

STRANGE COINCIDENCE

I contributed an article to the Northern Constitution newspaper on our visit to Calandar House and it successfully got through the censors and so I sent Miss Haddow a couple of copies. It's nice to mention that the lady had already been the recipient of a selection of Irish linen items from Brian.

Later, I changed from Army khaki to the blue of the Royal Air Force and was stationed at the 57 Operational Training Unit, Northumberland, 25 miles from the Tyneside City of Newcastle.

From the vast isolated R.A.F. station the nearest place of civilisation was the village of Felton, through which the River Coquet flows and it had large salmon runs each season. I managed to get a licence for ten shillings and enjoyed catching brown trout, but the big silver denizens were very much out-of-bounds to me.

I wasn't too long in getting mixed in Felton's entertainment circles for the forces and it was in the Community Hall that I met the

Village Parish Priest, Father Doherty, a native of Donegal. Not only was he a good organiser of concerts and musical evenings, but a skilled fly fisherman with permission to take salmon from the Coquet. I envied him.

In addition to helping out musically at Felton, I was guesting on saxophone two nights a week at a large dance hall named the Oxford Gallery in Newcastle and was on my way there one Easter Monday, when the sparse bus service had ceased to operate for some reason.

I was standing on the Main Road hitch-hiking a lift to the big city when, at last, a small blue van stopped and the lady driver in the blue uniform of the Voluntary Fire Service said: "I can give you a lift, but you will have to suffer the discomfort of the back."

Expressing thanks I jumped into the back of the vehicle and sat on a box well within speaking range of the lady. A gentleman in a lounge suit sat beside her. I was to learn later that he was a high ranking Army Officer on leave and was accompanying his wife on one of her tours of duty.

During the journey the lady kindly directed the conversation to me and I explained that I was serving in England for the first time and that I had transferred from the Army, having had a spell in Scotland.

"Which part of Scotland?" the lady asked.

"Grangemouth." I told her.

"We live near to there ... our home is in Falkirk." the lady said.

"Falkirk!" I exclaimed, "My officer and I had a great day at a pheasants shoot on Calandar House estate."

The lady pulled the van to a stop and turned and stared at me. "Calandar House is our home, but I'm presently stationed in Newcastle." she went on to explain.

Amazingly, I had been picked up by the Hon Mr and Mrs Forbes. The lady continued the journey and on arriving at their destination, a tall blackstone terraced house, I joined them there for coffee and saw a copy of my article on Calandar House, which Miss Haddow had sent.

Leaving the distinguished couple the gentleman spoke for the first time. "Oh my!" he ejaculated, "The world is not as big a place as we think it is."

A WHOPPER!

One morning the Station Administration Officer, Squadron Leader McFarland, approached me and said: "We have the Air Commodore coming tomorrow and have got him a few hours salmon fishing on the Coquet, will you act as gillie for him?"

"Certainly, sir," I replied, delighted at getting away from the boredom of ordinary daily duties, for a spell.

Next morning the Air Commodore commenced casting a pair of flies over a heavenly stretch of broken water with a borrowed fifteen foot rod and a stiff breeze blowing in his face didn't help his accurate landing of the flies in any way. Indeed, he was equivalent to a rookie on the Square with two left feet.

Yet, when the heavy stream took the flies down to the tail of a pool a fine silver fish rose to them and the angler was really excited. I suggested that he rested the fish for a few minutes and he agreed as a gillie once gave him that advice while fishing the River Wye.

He smoked a cigarette and then resumed fishing, but the fish never came again, simply because the flies never went anywhere near it. However, his miss was the main talking point in the mess that evening I was told.

My experiences on our Irish rivers had taught me that a rising fish to the fly is a taking fish, I decided to tie one of Pat Curry's fiery brown size 4 flies on a strong cast and take my 10ft splitcane rod and pursue the fish the Air Commodore had rose.

Next morning on the dot of five o'clock I cycled to the Coquet and, against all rules of the river, was soon casting the big fiery brown fly downstream and it was landing perfectly with hackles expressing themselves in true style. I was full of confidence.

At 6.10am I hooked the fish at the very spot it had showed on the previous day and it was a monster, which bent the little rod from the point to the cork handle. But I knew to keep the strain on and what line to give and what line to reel in and so on the hour of 7am I had the fish under control.

Then my heart missed a beat, for coming down the bank was an angler with a rod over his shoulder and a net in hand. It was Father Doherty.

"Father," I lied, almost breathless, "I was fishing for trout there and hooked this brute."

"Will you stop your blarney 'Speedy' and bring the fish in till I get the net under it." came the reply.

Not only did he keep quiet about my illegal catch, but delivered it safely to the Station, where I was waiting to sell the beauty to the Officers Mess.

At tea break in the Mess later that morning the salmon, fresh-run and weighing 19lb, was brought in on a silver platter and laid in front of the Air Commodore, who shouted aloud and in earnest: "That insolent Irishman stole my fish!"

He left at mid-day and I wasn't on the runway to wish him 'tight lines' for the future, as his plane took off.

That story of the two-faced cheeky Irish airman has appeared in various periodicals.

FINBAR

Finbar, from the mountain and I somehow managed to keep in touch during our spell in the forces, and when I was posted to Le Bouget Airport on the liberation of Paris, I learned that he was just 300 Kilometres from the metropolis.

At last we met for a weekend and though Paris exerted an interesting claim on our attention we mostly spoke about the old country and longed for the evening when we would have that reunion ceilidh and a drop of good poteen in the Donnelly cabin.

We embraced in tears and parted with that great forthcoming celebration in both our hearts. But it was not to be ... may the soil of Germany lie lightly on the broth 'o a boy.

Chapter TWELVE

HOME AGAIN IN 'CIVVY STREET' I JUST COULDN'T GET SETTLED INTO THE WAY OF THINGS. FIVE YEARS IN uniform moving from here to there had given me 'itchy' feet and, really, I could see no great future by staying in Northern Ireland. There was a bit of building work about, but that was out of my depth and somehow I couldn't get the pen or musical instruments into money-making action. As Aunt Mary Jane Moore once termed a similar situation involving me - I was in a rut!

All my life I had a fad to sail to Australia and see what things were like there. I had heard good reports, especially from a good friend, Major Harold Marcus Ervine- Andrews, whom I was accompanying on fishing trips to the two Agivey rivers and Dugan's Bay on the Bann estuary. In the last months of the war, he had been Directorate of Military Operations at Victoria Barracks, Melbourne, and knew a number of that city's influential people.

Here I must concede that I had a very healthy bank book, thanks to the Paris 'Black Market' which I knew the ins and outs of.

Dealings were shady admittedly, but British servicemen grabbed the opportunity to line their pockets as they were about to discard the uniform.

My wife Margaret had moved to a comfortable residence in Coleraine, so getting her permission to go to Australia to plan a future for her and our children, I booked a passage, making Melbourne my destination. It was then Harold kindly gave me a letter of introduction to his friends in the city. They would advise and help me.

Major Harold Marcus Ervine-Andrews was the first Irishman in the second world war to be awarded the Victoria Cross, the highest British Military Honour.

On the night of May 31st, 1940, when a Lieutenant in the East Lancashire Regiment, Harold took over a thousand yards of defences in front of Dunkirk. For over ten hours in the face of vastly superior forces, he and his company held their position. When there was a danger of one of the platoons being breached by the enemy he filled the gap with volunteers and advanced alone, holding the enemy with his rifle from the roof of a barn.

Although constantly bombarded, Harold accounted for seventeen of the enemy with his rifle and many more with a bren gun later handed to him. Though wounded four times he refused to stop firing until his ammunition finished. A great deed of valour.

FAREWELL

It was difficult saying another farewell to my ageing mother, who challenged me if I was doing the right thing going so far away in spec of a job. She wasn't too keen on me leaving my wife and children and I doubt if my alibi that it would be for their good in the end was accepted.

The dear woman wept sorely as I opened the door of her home to leave. Then through her tears she asked: "You have, of course, the wee Bible I gave you going to the war?"

"Oh yes, yes." I replied.

"Keep reading it son," she pleaded, "it's the only way."

I had lied again to my loving mother. I hadn't read a line of her wee Bible. It had lay at the bottom of my kitbag for the duration of the war .

That was my form as I boarded the liner 'Orontes' at Tilbury Docks. I was inclined to think more of what lay ahead rather than the sadness I had left behind in Ireland. I was a through-other character with the tendency to move on with my own inklings which, at times, weren't too sensible.

Soon the giant vessel had moved gracefully down the Thames to the open sea and was on her way to the Bay of Biscay. On arriving there she began to roll in the mountainous rough swells, which resulted in sea sickness becoming quite rife on board. The passengers not affected could be seen attending those who could hardly lift their heads. That part of the voyage is best forgotten.

Much more pleasant was the Mediterranean, which came next. There the smooth deep blue sea and the setting sun in the horizon provided a colour scene, which had all passengers on the upper deck beholding the spectacle. Really, beauty beyond adequate description.

Fuel was obtained at Port Said and then after ten hours crawling along the narrow Canal, the vessel entered the Gulf of Suez and from there it was a long stretch of uninterrupted sailing during which passengers played deck games and bathed in the pool.

The long promenade deck served well in giving me a good morning constitutional and that was very necessary, for I spent most of my evenings in the bar, where duty-free drinks could be bought for a few pence and I ruthlessly abused the concession.

By now the passengers had got to know each other and when they congregated on the upper deck the place was like a little township with its 'titters' of gossip should anyone step out of place. But when the various destinations were reached, everlasting friendships had been made and partings brought tears.

LAND AT LAST

Melbourne presented some striking features to me. I was surprised at its vast proportions, it having been founded only in 1835. All public buildings were substantially built and tastefully designed. And the city also had a fine selection of parks and indoor Leisure Centres.

I was fortunate in finding 'digs' at Barrington Guest House and while there had an unusual, but pleasant experience. One evening while reading a magazine in the sitting room a fellow guest asked me where I came from.

"Coleraine," I answered.

"Coleraine!" he exclaimed, showing interest. "Which part?"

"Lilac Avenue," I replied.

"Never heard of it," returned the other, "and I've lived in Coleraine all of my life."

"Lilac Avenue is not too long built," I explained, "maybe it wasn't there when you came to Australia."

"What do you mean man? I was born in Australia and I am an Australian." the fellow said noticeably confused.

Then another guest, a Lurgan man, came to our rescue. Pointing to me smiling he said: "You come from Coleraine in Ireland and this gentleman is from Coleraine in south west Victoria. Both of you have got a bit mixed up, but it has been good fun listening to the pair of you."

The Australian rose from his chair and came over to me with outstretched hand. "Brother!" he said joyfully, "Leave it there, you're the first person from old Mother Coleraine I've ever met. You are welcome to our country."

The Coleraine Australian was named Arthur Barton and he was extremely proud of his Irish heritage. He produced a document. "Burkes Landed Gentry In Ireland" which referred to his family as one of the most noted. Celebrated members were Samuel Barton, the greatest barrister in Irish history and Sir Thomas Plunkett Barton, a judge of the High Court of Ireland. Kesh, County Fermanagh, is the original Barton country.

Some years later, Arthur visited Kesh and also spent a couple of days in the Bannside territory of old Mother Coleraine.

In time I called on Harold Ervine-Andrews friends, which included newspaper editors, government officials, radio presenters and a retired sea captain. Then I had a look around the city and its districts and on failing to find anything like the homliness that prevailed in the old country, I wondered if my wife and children could possibly adapt themselves to this standoffish way of living. I very much doubted it, for I wasn't too fussy about it.

Truthfully, my expensive venture had been a big mistake. In fact, a total disaster and now my selfish dominance wasn't going to give my wife and children the chance of seeing Australia and choosing for themselves whether or not they liked it. In a bullying attitude I had to get doing everything my way.

I strolled around for a few days and if there had been a bridge from Australia to any part of Europe I would have been on it walking and really glad to be doing so. But that was not to be. I had made my bed here and would have to lie on it.

The money I had brought was running out. I was now down to drinking wine. It was only three shillings for a ten-glass bottle and my bedroom at the 'digs' was full of them.

Before leaving home for Australia I had faithfully promised to do articles for the Chronicle of immigrants from within the paper's precincts and, of course, anything of interest. But for the sake of readers stomachs and my own, there is one observation I never would have described and that was the plight of 'wineos' I encountered on the banks of the River Yarra in Melbourne. Their dreadful appearance and filthy habits were quite unbelievable.

The road to despair, and finally hell, opened up for those men and women when as unsuspecting boys and girls they accepted a seemingly innocent glass of sherry or sparkling champagne.

I sympathised with them, yet here I was swallowing the dope, glass after glass, that had wrecked them. It was then I realised that if I was going to remain sane and get back to Ireland in one piece, I would have to find a job and raise the price of the passage.

Looking the paper I saw a job that appealed to me. A building firm required labourers to work on a Hydroelectric Scheme, many miles from Melbourne. That afternoon I went along to the employment office and was warmly accepted into the open arms of a Sligo man, John Tumulty, who implied that a border may separate us on the old green sod, but in Australia we were strongly united Irishmen.

Tumulty was a kind-of ganger-administrator and at one time hadn't only kissed the Blarney Stone, but had taken a big bite out of it. He was full of Irishisms.

But the one thing I liked about his patriotism, he got me a seat beside the driver in the truck taking us to the job, while the twenty other slaves, speaking different languages, were packed like sardines in the rear department.

MUSIC ON THE BRAIN

I was finding the handling of a shovel, pick and spade tough and already was counting the days until I had my boat fare saved. But I was determined to stick it out, for I had written to wife Margaret that I was coming home.

The accommodation comprised makeshift wooden huts, with two labourers billeted in one. I was most fortunate in having a hut all to myself, maybe another gesture of Tumulty's. The privacy suited me, for I was writing articles for the Chronicle.

Tumulty had invited me to play the banjo in the large canteen some evenings and everyone seemed to enjoy the sessions as they drank beer.

The banjo, a zither with a small solid mahogany vellum casing, was the only instrument I had at the camp. Being wise for once I left the saxophone and other valuables in the safe custody of the Melbourne 'digs'.

Staffed by more than 200 cosmopolitan workers the camp was an agreeable enough place only for one character who, continually, kept upsetting things. An Australian born monster of 6ft 4ins he considered those of us not Australian to be 'runners' and impostors and was very loud-mouthed in declaring it. His nickname was 'Tripe' but strictly that was uttered behind his back. He was an obnoxious bullying scoundrel and everyone on the camp from the bosses down were scared of him.

One evening in the canteen I was playing a request for Tumulty 'I'll Take You Home Again Kathleen' and it was touching his heart as his wife was named Kathleen. Then suddenly, 'Tripe', coming from the bar area holding a pint of beer in his hand towered over me and shouted: "Hi! Cut out that sob stuff here. When in Aussie land you play what the Aussies want. Give us 'Matilda' and I mean now!"

As I was on the last bars of 'Kathleen' I played on intending to break into 'Matilda' directly on finishing the Irish gem. But I could see 'Tripe' leaving his glass on the bar counter and coming towards me in a threatening manner. Rising from my chair I swung the banjo over my right shoulder it came down on the head of the person whom I assumed was going to attack me. A self-defence action which had contacted perfectly and left the recipient out cold on the floor.

Fortunately, the sick bay attendant was present and rendered first aid. But his appeal for a couple of stretcher bearers to take 'Tripe' to sick bay met with no response and so in the end, Tumulty and I did the removal, and I was shaking with fear, for there was no sign of the hulk recovering consciousness.

But news reached me the next day that he had come round and having received eleven stitches was being confined to sick-bay for at least four days. The big joke was that the patient was suffering from music on the brain.

But, apart from the funny side, there was quite some concern in camp circles as to what 'Tripe's' reaction would be to being banjoed when he returned to work. The general opinion was that he would be seeking revenge with violence.

Tumulty had completely lost his sense of humour through worrying about me and I wasn't too happy. Dear old Tumulty advised me to pack up and leave before 'Tripe' made his appearance. He even assured me of another job on the other side of Melbourne far away from the brute.

But I decided to stay and take the consequences. I couldn't act the coward by running away, especially now that I was being acclaimed a hero in camp.

I had chummed up with a wartime R.A.F. fighter pilot who answered to the name Michael Bennett, from Dublin, an adventurous fellow who was on a working tour of Australia. He was sitting beside me at breakfast the morning 'Tripe' entered the dining block, his head well bandaged. Looking all around he spotted me and then made his way up to where I sat. I could hear the loud thumps of my heart on my chest and I'm sure Michael could also hear them.

But, surprisingly, 'Tripe' didn't blare and gulder in his usual manner, but was reasonably calm when he said: "Paddy, you had no real cause to hit me with your banjo the other evening ... you've left me with a very nasty head."

Staring at him, I replied firmly: "You can be thankful it wasn't a two-edged sword I had or you wouldn't be here this morning. Who are you to think you have the liberty to humiliate decent human beings as if they were dirt?"

'Tripe' walked timidly from my presence without reply and on collecting breakfast sat eating alone. To the lookers-on of that little morning scene, the fellow workers he had so often intimidated, he had proved himself not only a big bag of hot air, but a fake and a coward.

I haven't included that story to make a hero of myself. My spell at Killowen school many years back taught me that the best policy when facing threatening bullies was to hit hard first. In the 'Tripe' affray I wasn't a super brave person nor one showing an example of the fighting Irish. As the bully, exhibiting his brawn, came at me I was petrified, but knew that if there was to be the slightest chance of survival for my much lighter and less muscular stature, I would have to get that vital first hit in. Thankfully, my beloved banjo was at hand to provide it.

Sadly the instrument was broken at the shaft, but a smith-engineer superbly put it together again. A silver-steel plate on the back of the resonator was inscribed. "Repaired by Thomas Reid, formerly of Ballinahinch, in memory of the glorious victory this banjo achieved for a tortured work force in Australia."

SYDNEY BLUNDER

Chatting in the canteen one evening over a pint of beer, Michael Bennett informed me that on next pay day he was packing in the job and heading for Sydney, where he was sure to get a ship on which to work his passage home. He had come abroad that way and after having seen most of New Zealand and Australia, he had had enough.

Michael's plan soon snowballed to my way of thinking. By relying on his experience of getting around I could be home in no time and it wouldn't cost me a penny. He didn't hesitate to agree when I said I would like to join him.

On pay day we both left the camp and were lucky to get a lift to Melbourne on a truck belonging to the firm. There I collected my belongings at the 'digs' and after selling the lot with the exception of the banjo, Michael and I booked on a train named the 'Spirit of Progress' and soon we started a three day journey to Sydney in quest of any kind of ship going to a European port.

Arriving in the vast city we spent a couple of days looking around and sleeping in a park at night. That was when I encountered

Australian bull ants for the first time and they weren't pleasant creatures, believe me. They seemed to like me much more than they did Michael and I had the bites to show for proof.

On the third day we went to the docks area and Michael knew exactly where to go for information of shipping departures. At last we found one. The 'Delidga' from Norway, a 3,000 ton cargo vessel was leaving in four days time.

We found the 'Delidga' and also the skipper, who, on hearing what we wanted, asked in broken English. "You have both got experience of seamanship?"

"Yes," lied Michael.

"Right," said the skipper, "You can have a free passage to Bergen, a bunk each, free drink and tobacco allowance and a third of the wages when we berth at port, on the condition that you start work now ... there's a bit of tidying-up on board to do ... eh?"

"That's fine with us." Michael assured him.

The first day in service we brushed and scrubbed the deck and made a satisfactory job of it. Feeling joyous and secure that evening I wrote a letter to my wife finishing with the rather sheepish postscript. "I'll be walking in the door one of these days to give you and the kids a big hug and kiss."

On the third morning the skipper's mate handed us paint brushes and scrapers, plus two lengths of rope and a wood plank with the words: "There's a couple of bare spots on the starboard side of ship, which the captain would like covered before we pull out on full tide tomorrow."

Michael had his way of getting the plank down to the spots with us sitting on each side of it, a precarious situation indeed. On the peril of our lives I had to hold on to the end of the rope with my left hand and start scraping with my right hand. The paint was lowered down to us and so after performing something like a balancing circus act we got the paint on the spots.

But on coming up towards the deck, carelessly and stupidly, I let my end of the rope slip out of my hands and as the plank and I hurtled downwards a dozen thoughts of fate raced through my mind.

I splashed deep into the water and took several sickening mouthfuls of it before breaking the surface. I could swim well thanks to the River Bann's free tuition in my birthday suit, so there was no immediate danger of me drowning.

Looking up I could see Michael dangling on the rope and several of the crew leaning over the deck rail directly above him laughing their heads off. Some joke!

We were to sail at 4pm on the great day of days, but during morning fatigues we learned from a hushed voice aboard that a lot of the ship's crew had deserted her at Freemantle.

Though that was disturbing news, it didn't altogether disillusion us, until, mercifully, we got another tip-off that we would be sailing and trading via Panama, a scheduled eighteen month voyage before reaching Bergen. In a matter of minutes we too had deserted the tub.

But it was like walking from the frying pan into the fire, for here we were in Sydney with very little money. Then things went even worse for me. Michael saw a job advertised in New Guinea. He applied and got it and I couldn't deny him the opportunity, for the appointment guaranteed a huge wage with expenses.

As I wandered round Sydney with its masses of cosmopolitan people, I was terribly lonely and homesick. Honestly, if I may use the virtuous word, I would have given my left arm to have been in homely Coleraine or Aghadowey. I wondered if ever I would see those homely places again.

Then when I sat in a railway station sipping at a mug of coffee, bought by my last few pence and dreading yet another night with the bull ants, a miracle happened. I turned my head in response to a tap on the shoulder and there stood a smart navy man with HMAS Sydney printed on his cap band. It was Jack McCloy from old Killowen.

Pointing to my dishevelled head and face he said: "I didn't recognise you, it was the old banjo I noticed. I would never have missed it after the great nights it gave us dancing on Bannside with the Scottish holiday-makers."

Jack had transferred from the Royal Navy to the Australian Navy and had just returned from the Korean War, where his ship had been in action. He took me along to a pub and put a few whiskeys under my belt, and during the process he slipped a fiver into my pocket - a fiver I never forgot.

Later, after a hefty meal of steak and onions, Jack escorted me to Paramatta, to the home of former Coleraine man Bob Cameron and his Australian wife, Chris. The kindly couple steeped me in a bath and as I lay that night between clean linen sheets in a comfortable bed looking out of the window at the star-filled sky of the Southern Cross, my mother came to mind. Could her constant prayers on my behalf have anything to do with today's fortunate happening? Then thranly I closed my eyes telling myself not to be silly.

Six months later I left Sydney docks, on the 'Orrontes' and in six weeks arrived back in Coleraine penniless and empty-handed and even without the old banjo. It had to go in an effort to raise my boat fare. Now the question has got to be asked: "Was I a wiser man?" Time will provide the answer.

Chapter
THIRTEEN

GOOD JOBS CONTINUED TO BE NON-EXISTENT IN
NORTH-WEST ULSTER IN THE FORTIES, SO I HAD NO
alternative, but to cross the Channel to Gloucester, England, and
start work in an R.A.F. Maintenance Unit. I had got a room in a
large industrial hostel, at Brockworth, four miles from the historic
city and varied tongues could be heard at the mass of tables including Welsh and Irish,

A gang of big strong drain-digging Connemara men conversed
continually in their native language and it was nice listening to them
though I didn't understand a word they spoke nor had the slightest
idea of what they were discussing.

I had brought my typewriter in a bag over my shoulder with the
hope of getting a few good-selling stories and, I did! I fed with a
crowd of Northern and Southern Irishmen, the majority of whom
were McAlpine's Fusiliers, Wimpey's Warriors, Costain-John
Brown's Crusaders, Kelly's Spidermen, McNicholl's Spacemen,
Sweeny's Mudlarks and McArthur's Braves and such was their

humour and anecdotes that a column emerged 'Around The Irish Table' which appeared in periodicals north and south of the border, including The Pink (Ireland's Saturday Night), Coleraine Chronicle, Northern Constitution and Cork Examiner.

I enjoyed writing those little human-interest stories and rejoiced so much at the letters I received from readers touched by them that I have selected a few from my treasured archives for this final narrative.

THE SMALL DARK MAN

The long table, of course, had its oddities and one of them sat at the very end, seemingly trying to edge himself into as much seclusion as possible. His accent proclaimed him a native of Belfast and I quickly assessed the fact that I had never known a strange miserable character such as he to come from the Lagan city. Any folk from there I had mixed with were exceptionally liberal and sociable.

Hostel residents referred to him as 'The Small Dark Man' and considered him the most stingy person on earth. He neither smoked nor drank, nor stood himself a bite of supper nor bought a newspaper nor treated himself to an evening at the hostel cinema, which was cheap. Instead, when off duty, he made the wireless room his headquarters. He wouldn't even pay his bus fare to work. but cycled there in all weathers on an old push bike and was a glutton for overtime. His lunch was always a couple of slices of bread taken from the hostel breakfast table.

I had heard him called 'A confounded miser,' and 'A disgrace to Ireland'. Daily, particularly from the Irish, he was bombarded with hate remarks, for it was rumoured that he had thousands of pounds in the bank and that his life's desire was to add to them while denying himself the slightest comfort. In the end I believed some of the rumours and disliked the wee man though he did me no harm nor anyone else to my knowledge.

Then one day the 'small dark man' sent for me. He was confined to his room with flu. I went along to find him not only ill, but worried.

"Will you do me a favour?" he asked, "I feel I can trust you."

"If it's in my power." I replied.

Reaching a hand under his pillow he produced a fat envelope and said: "Please register this at Gloucester Head Post Office and bring me back the receipt."

On the way to the Post Office I stole a glance at the envelope and noticed that it was addressed to a male namesake of the 'small dark man.' My curiosity was tense.

Returning with the receipt I sat on the edge of the sick man's bed. "You say very little," I said, "and you act rather mysteriously ... aren't you going to tell me something about yourself?"

"There's little to tell," he replied and his tone was solemn. "Four years ago I lost my dear wife Annie, then shortly afterwards had the misfortune to be paid off my job in Belfast. My responsibilities were heavy, so I had to leave home and find work here."

"You say your responsibilities were heavy ... in what way?" I asked.

"My two sons are studying at Queen's University," he explained, "If everything goes well Edward is due to qualify in medicine next year and Tony in engineering the year after." Then noticeably distressed, he added: "I hope this illness of mine doesn't last too long. It would be disastrous if my sons great chance in life should be lost now."

That night every Irish hat within the precincts of Brockworth Hostel was lifted high to a brave father and a great Ulsterman!

O'RILEY

Another person we figured to be an oddity at the table was O'Riley. He hailed from west Donegal and wasn't much of an ambassador for that lovely part of our country nor the warm-hearted people there. He was a poor mixer and certainly no one showed any desire to mix with him. And wherever he went in the dining hall disgusted eyes followed his movements and there was general wonderment as to how such a creature was permitted into decent clean society. The rags he wore were filthy and the patched wellingtons on his feet had long since lost their heels. And he had nothing else to replace them with. Absolutely nothing!

O'Riley was known to the tablers as the 'long distance man,' a character who faced the physical hazards of the road, a social outcast, living only for a quart of scrumpy (cider) and a bottle of 'meth' to top it up. I could clearly discern by his suffused countenance that he was a sad hopeless victim of alcohol.

The long distance man had received temporary employment from a Costain-John Brown foreman, John Ryan, who had known his brother Ronan and so he wanted to help the wreck get some nourishing food and a few pounds.

Chris told me that O'Riley had arrived to work in England a clean, temperance-loving, chapel-going youth, but had fallen by the wayside through taking that first glass of cider.

I remember well the morning the manager called O'Riley from the breakfast table and told him he would have to leave the hostel immediately not because of his raggy filthy clothes, but for the unbearable stink he left after using the toilets. It was making the staff and residents sick.

O'Riley, a bit downhearted, finished in the job at Cheltenham and headed off. Around the table that evening a talkative fellow said to Chris: "O'Riley's gone and it's a good riddance!"

"I don't know," Chris replied, "such was the snow and frosty conditions of the road this morning that none of my squad would attempt to do the two mile walk to the little store for the eats for our tea break and lunch and I couldn't blame them. But it was then O'Riley volunteered to take on the task and so I gave him the exact money for the items required. He returned in good time and was almost frozen. I noticed that he had three loafs of bread instead of two. 'Why three loaves when I just ordered two?' I questioned."

"The shivering man looked at me and retorted: "On such a cruel morning the birds have got to eat as well as you and me."

There was silence at the table for the duration of dinner.

The last news we heard of the long distance man was that he was killed by a car on the road he had known well for so many years - the road to the 'big smoke.'

KINDLY BOYLE

The table was not without its jesters and prominent among them was Paddy Boyle, from Foxford, County Mayo. He was a real artiste at telling stories, not always authentic, mind you, but enjoyable.

There was a pub in Gloucester, beside the Guild Hall, with an Irish flavour, The boss was an Irishman, his assistants were Irish and most of his customers were Irish.

One Saturday evening when Boyle was present having a pint, brogues from every corner of the oul' green sod could be heard.

But suddenly the blethering of tongues ceased as a fine looking big priest, complete with umbrella, walked into the pub. Immediately a passage was made for him up through the throng to the bar counter, where he ordered a Guinness and a glass of Irish whiskey.

As his reverence was about to pay for the order, big-hearted Boyle, a regular mass worshipper, jumped forward, pushed a five-pound note into the barman's hand. "I'll pay for that," he said, bubbling over with excitement.

Then after the priest had swallowed both drinks, the good Samaritan said: "Would you have the same again?"

"I will indeed my son." answered the priest.

And when the second lot was put out of sight, the priest lifted his gloves to depart when Boyle said with appeal: "I couldn't force you to have another couple? I know I'll be rewarded for it."

"Thank you very much my son, I've just got time for another couple." the priest said with a smile.

At the end of the session Boyle escorted him down to the door and it was then he said: "Your face is strange, where's your parish?"

"Parish my foot!" returned the other, "I'm playing the part of Father O'Flynn in a play in the Guild Hall. This is the interval. I must go and resume - thanks for the drinks."

ENGLISH ROSE

Quite a number of boys and girls resided in the hostel, solely to explore in their spare time the glorious Cotswolds. Jack Harrison and his pretty young wife Dorothy were tremendously keen on this form of recreation and most weekends could seen setting off on their bicycles.

This devoted and charming Yorkshire couple spurned the responsibility of domestication and found in the hostel, apart from its delightful situation, freedom.

Jack, a draughtsman and Dorothy, a short-hand typist in the Hawker Siddeley Group, often gave us the pleasure of their company at The Irish Table and they continually got me talking about Australia, for they had planned a cycle tour of that country. I said they would enjoy every minute of their visit and wished them well. Of course, I omitted telling them of the terrible mess I made of what should have been a really successful and enjoyable trip.

Jack and Dorothy would spend hours thrilling us with their travelling experiences and so we became inseparable friends and showed our appreciation by bringing them gifts from Ireland. In our eyes the couple were very special.

Then Jack and Dorothy arranged a European tour as a training stunt for their great Australia venture. The day came for them to leave us, but it was not an unhappy parting, for we knew that this was their life - movement and change.

The cycle tour from Gloucestershire to Southern England was uneventful. There they boarded a ship for Spain. Then when they were nearing that sun-baked paradise, tragedy cruelly struck! Dorothy became ill and died!

Today the pride of Yorkshire rests in Spain. Her grave is marked by a tombstone of very ordinary design and bears a brief inscription. Unassuming to the end, she had wished for such simplicity. But in my heart and in the hearts of any Irish tablers still alive there is a more exalted memorial - a memorial to a lovely English rose the garden of the world could scarcely afford to lose.

PADDY SMIDDY

I had parted from the R.A.F. Maintenance Unit, for a more lucrative job in the Brockworth Engineering Company, which was producing the Sapphire jet aero engine. After considerable training I had qualified as a machine operator.

At lunchtime most of the employees went outside for a mouthful of fresh air and a few minutes relaxation. I followed this procedure as indoor confinement never seemed to agree with me.

Once when going through the factory gates I heard someone whistling my favourite tune, 'Dear Old Donegal.' It came from the lips of a tall thin man in blue boiler suit. Pulled well down the right side of his face was a green beret. He was a distance up the road and by the time I got there he was joined by a mate and the pair had set off, probably for a snack.

I carried on until it was time to turn and wander back to work. Nearing the factory strains of a mouth organ reached my ears. Glancing over my shoulder I discovered that the instrumentalist was the tall thin man and the lively tune he played was 'Tipperary.'

Behind him and his mate marched a crowd of singing Gloucestershire men, who were known to me. I was amazed! Who was this super minstrel with the power to break down such a barrier of reserve?

During the afternoon at my machine I mused over the parade and the talent of the minstrel and my imagination was fired with possibility of an interesting story for the press.

Lifting a tool I went to the store more as an excuse to find the whereabouts of my minstrel more than anything else. I found him operating a high-speed machine with a drill barely thicker than a needle. With split-second precision his long tapering fingers would reach in beneath the tool to retract the finished component and insert another.

When the smart operator had completed a batch of components, I approached him. "Good day." I greeted.

"And good day to you my good and worthy friend." he replied in a fascinating thick brogue, unmistakingly that of County Cork.

He stopped the machine and faced me. I met his eyes and held them keenly - large brown peculiar eyes. Then I realised the stark truth. They were sightless eyes!

I fought to suppress my emotion knowing well that it would only tend to embarrass one so afflicted. But my effort was unnecessary, for sensing my discomfiture the blind man produced a packet of cigarettes and said: "Have a woodbine."

As I accepted, a feeling of reassurance possessed me and I said: "You come from County Cork?"

"I do and I'm proud of the fact." he replied.

"Is it long since you were home?" I asked.

"Eight years and it seems like a lifetime." He paused, took a couple of draws from his cigarette and continued: "My wife and I were going home on holiday four years ago when I totally lost my sight without warning."

"Terrible!" I exclaimed and then wondered whether or not I had said the right thing.

But the blind man smiled and said: "You people blessed with your sight may think so, but it's really not so bad if a victim has the courage to resign himself to the cruel act of fate. Life to me is still something I enjoy and the sightless can be quite useful to society, thanks to the training schemes of today."

Stepping forward, his hand found my shoulder and he went on: "And we can sometimes reciprocate the help you folk give us and to prove it I'll softly sing a wee song I've composed.

"When the night is dark and fog descends,
You know not where to go,
For you with vision strong and good,
The hopes are very low.
The blind man knows by instinct
The way to his abode,
And you've no such second sight
To guide you on the road.
You're lost and well you know it,
You've nothing left to do
But pray that some blind man may come
And lead the way for you."

My heart filled with admiration for this man, who later explained that his name was Paddy Smiddy.

I was soon to discover that as well as the mouth organ my new-found-friend was a tin whistler of tremendous skill, so I borrowed a five-string banjo and we gave a performance of Irish tunes in the factory social club one evening which earned the applause of everyone present.

After having played the 'Wearin' O' The Green' by request I leaned over the table towards Paddy and said in good humour: "You wouldn't by any chance know a wee tune called 'The Sash My Father Wore?"

The Cork minstrel's face lit up in a broad smile as he replied: "Man I do!" Then holding up the tin whistle he went on: "And this wee girl should be able to play it, for I received her six years ago from a northern orange man."

That is the simple story of a simple man, who had the great courage to overcome a sudden descent into total darkness and live with it and at the same time make people happy.

Chapter FOURTEEN

I HAD COME BACK TO COLERAINE TO WRITE FOR THE CHRONICLE AND SOLICIT FOR ADVERTISING ON A freelance basis, one of a team intent on enlarging the paper's circulation and, thankfully, we succeeded through paying no attention to the clock and getting on with the job.

My human-interest stories and features were being well received by the paper's readership and as well I had a summer engagement playing music each evening in a Portrush Hotel, having reequipped myself with a banjo and saxophone.

Indeed, I was a very busy person seeking writing material in different parts of Counties Antrim and Derry, in a little van, which I also used to take me to the evening music sessions.

But how thrifty was I with my considerable earnings? Did I transform them into a hive of prosperity? No. I was still drinking, whiskey preferably and that proved to be rather expensive.

I should, perhaps, have adapted a more cautious and sensible attitude towards the risk of developing the habit after having been face to face with the Australian wineo plight and the scrumpy addict, O'Riley, in Gloucester. But I had fully convinced myself that I could never become a dreadful stinking wreck, similar to them. No! Never!

My form of drinking, I figured, was helping my work. Having a couple gave me a kind-of passport into a pub and as I stated earlier in this narrative, there is no better place in the world for finding interesting characters. In fact, I made certain pubs my landmark in the towns and villages I visited from time to time.

On my return to Coleraine, mother had offered me back the writing space in her home and I accepted. In addition to that dullness of eye and reddish-purple flush of the nose-point and cheeks steady whiskey drinking causes, it had now further marked me with an enlarged midriff and jaws. But, fortunately, my Lady of Long Commons never referred to the disfigurements. Seemingly, she was too glad seeing her wee Willie back home and showing keen interest in his writing and music.

Mother's constant companion was the Bible and the one thing I feared was her bringing up the question again of the wee Bible she had given me going to the war and which she thought was my spiritual guide in Australia and England.

Somehow, I didn't like telling her lies that I still had the Bible and was reading its pages, when it was nowhere to be found! And, of course, I wanted to keep from her the fact that I no longer believed in the Scriptures she had once taught me nightly.

The shrewd woman, a reader of the 'Christian Herald' and the Salvation Army's 'Young Soldier' had established her own ministry for attacking alcoholism. Any articles she saw in the 'Herald' or 'Soldier' on the subject she would cut out and leave for me to consider whether or not they were worthy of reprinting in my Chronicle articles. However, I knew the literature was left for me alone to digest.

Sister Annie told me one day when we were alone that mother hadn't given up hope of me taking to the temperance trail. Annie constantly heard the dear woman pray aloud nightly for my sobriety and salvation. My answer to this statement was a shrug of the shoulders and the retort: "I'm a grown man now with a wife and family and should be treated as such."

Arriving at Long Commons to begin work one morning I picked up a 'Young Soldier' cutting and it contained this assessment of alcohol addiction from the pen of Evangeline Booth. "Drink has drained more blood, hung more crepe, filled more coffins, sold more homes, armed more villains, slain more children, stripped more wedding rings, twisted more limbs, dethroned more reasons, wrecked more manhood, dishonoured more womanhood, broken more hearts and driven more victims to suicide, than any other evil that ever swept the world."

Before turning to my typewriter I gave thought to Evangeline's strong condemnation of something that is meant to be stimulating, comforting and affable. Certainly there would be despair for those who abused it like O'Riley. I was using it for business, social and relaxation and music purposes. And though I wouldn't be jumping on the temperance trail mother prayed for and hoped for, she need not worry in the slightest about me going over the brink. I was too well prepared against that ever happening.

DAISY

I always found it nice going to a house, where a bottle of spirits or wine was put on the table. A long interview without the gesture had the danger of turning to boredom. But there was one home in the suburbs of Coleraine I remember entering and I hardly expected such hospitality. Let me explain.

A young housewife had died suddenly and all kinds of rumours were floating round the borough as to what caused her death, some of them nasty.

A Chronicle assistant editor asked me to call on the parents of the deceased and get authentic details of the tragedy and do an obituary for Thursday afternoon's paper if, of course, the bereaved wished it.

The parents didn't want anything in the paper about their daughter, yet, strange enough, they brought me inside their comfortable home and over a cup of tea revealed the cause of her death and it wasn't pleasant.

Daisy, a real puritan and ex-girl guide, was closely connected with the activities of her church and worshipped there at every opportunity. It was within church circles that she met Jim, which proved to be a case of love at first sight. The young pair were inseparable.

When they got engaged they began saving for a bungalow and both being exceptionally energetic and thrifty they eventually acquired one fully furnished in a nice part of the borough.

Daisy had a beautiful white wedding and she looked so girlish, pretty and glowing at the reception in a posh Portrush hotel.

When the 140 guests were seated at the tables, the wine waiter had already left two glasses of sherry in front of the bride and groom for the toasts. Jim could take or leave a sherry but Daisy had never tasted the stuff in her life and had no notion of doing so.

But, alas, the best man kept urging the bride to take the sherry to toast the happiest day of her life and it was then her eyes fell upon the clergyman sitting at the end of the top table. He had already finished his sherry and was holding his glass out for a refill.

"If he can take two then I can take one." she whispered to herself.

And so Daisy had her first alcoholic beverage and as she finished it there were cheers of 'bravo' from the guests adjacent to her. Then came more toasts and fill-ups.

After returning from honeymoon the couple moved into their bungalow and were gloriously happy.

In the weeks that followed, genial Daisy was to meet three other young housewives, Eileen, Judith and Jane, who lived near to her. Each morning the four ladies would congregate, taking it in turn to entertain and at the coffee tables they would discuss different matters.

But one morning Eileen produced a bottle of sherry and offered to treat her good friends. They accepted and the internal glow of the drug seemed to make the get-together more lively and homely.

While shopping that afternoon, Daisy decided to reciprocate Eileen's nice gesture as she had her friends the next morning. And so it went on and on until Daisy got the taste of gin and soda water and she was having four large ones a day.

The neighbourly get-togethers had now become tame affairs and she no longer attended them to the wondering of Eileen, Judith and Jane. What had happened to Daisy?

Eventually, Daisy's kitchen resembled a miniature bar and on Jim objecting strongly, the young wife, using the deep cunning alcohol craving instils in its victims, started hiding bottles in all kinds of places and at the same time kept trying to hide her grave problem, thus jeopardising her chance of vital treatment.

Foolishly, an embarrassed Jim also tried to keep his wife's problem within the precincts of the bungalow and that was a grave mistake.

Daisy's love for Jim had now completely foundered and that resulted in the sad husband going back to live with his parents. The only thing Daisy had any love for was that bottle with the pretty label. And she obtained them daily through an ordering system.

Poor broken Daisy's debts had now got so much out of control that the bank was preparing to take over the bungalow. Her parents, clergyman, and friends had tried in every way to help the alcoholic, but the only time she allowed them into her home was when they brought her drink, which she had to have to keep her from going completely mad.

On the eve of the authorities coming to put Daisy into care of which she knew nothing, she had agreed to her parents request to stay in the bungalow overnight.

The parents saw their daughter to bed with ample drink and going into the next room dozed over asleep. On wakening some hours later they went into the daughter's room to discover her missing. And surprisingly, the drink hadn't been touched.

Then to their horror they had a sniff of gas. Rushing downstairs they found that Daisy, their cherished darling, had taken the easy way out - the gas oven!

While not wanting anything about their daughter to appear in the paper beyond a simple notice, why did the parents pass on the gruesome details of her death to me? Later I was to learn that the bereaved couple had joined a White Ribbon Temperance Campaign and were counselling people with a drink problem, so that Daisy may not have died in vain. They had on their list a fellow named 'Speedy' Moore, who was said to be drinking a fair bit over the limit and a splendid opportunity had arose to talk to him, through the brain plan of a church-going editor, whose wife and sister were White Ribboners.

But did their pitiful form of counselling deter me and lessen my drinking or cease it altogether? No. On the contrary I retained my defensive stand for the booze and put Daisy down as an easy-led fool and weakling. I saw her as a senseless chicken to have allowed herself to have fallen into such a degrading state and then finish up in the role of coward by taking her own life. If you can't hold a drop of drink, the alternative is simple. Don't touch it!

Tall words, indeed! And spoken by a person who himself, was now relying on a streak of cunning to hide his own drinking from folk close to him, particularly his wife and mother.

GRANSHA

I was now finding that a couple of glasses of gin first thing in the morning lifted me a bit and I chose gin because going afterwards to my mother's to work, it was less smelling than whiskey.

Of course, I didn't go to a Coleraine pub for this starter, where tale-carrying sneaks may have been lurking, but motored the short distance to the privacy of the Village Inn, Articlave.

One memorable morning when the boss of the inn was on duty we got talking. And we had lots to talk about, for he was a grandson of the famous Professor Sam Fleming, earlier mentioned in this narrative.

But the genial landlord was quick to change the conversation when he saw my hands shaking a bit and went on to query his observation with some concern.

"I'll be as right as rain when I get a couple of gins down me," I said smiling, "I admit to having a hangover after last night in the hotel I had been playing music in."

On me finishing the second drink, Richard said: "James is here now to take over the bar, would you like to come to my home for a few minutes, it's most important?"

I agreed to discover that my host was an official of Alcoholic Anonymous, set on asking me a number of questions which I felt I was compelled to answer truthfully, for here was someone I really trusted.

The questions over, Richard made a mug of coffee and as we sipped he shook me to the very core when he said: "I've bad news for you 'Speedy,' you are an addict requiring immediate treatment!"

I sat starring at him as he went on: "There is a good chance of recovery if you join A.A. and accept our doctrine. You will meet dozens of men and women in the same plight as you and they will render valuable help to your efforts to remain sober. What do you say?"

Pondering over the matter I realised that the only alternative I had was to say yes - in the meantime anyway.

Further encouraged by Richard I did attend A.A. and surprised many folk by abstaining from strong drink for two weeks. But I had doubled my cigarette smoking and at work in mother's home my thoughts were continually with the pub at the end of the street. I wasn't at all happy, not a bit of me.

Then a big test came. An important organisation was having its Convention in a Portrush Hotel and the Chronicle had received an invitation to attend the final evening's dinner and who better was there to do a write-up on the function than a steady and sober 'Speedy' Moore?

But I never got a line written about that function. Just before dinner was served a tray of sherry came round the guests and members of press. "One wouldn't do me any harm." I whispered to myself, so I yielded to temptation.

After draining the glass I, somewhat unconsciously, wandered to the hotel bar and from that moment on I have only faint recollections of the entire weekend.

On the Monday morning the Rev Brian Liddell and A.A. worker, George Stinson, were called upon to transport me to Londonderry's Mental Asylum, Gransha, where I did a drying-out period.

Though places like Gransha were indispensable, folk in the old days were inclined to look upon a person who spent a spell in one, whatever the ailment, as not quite twelve pence to the shilling.

People, who normally would have stopped me on the street for a chat, were now rushing past with a nod of the head. There was, of course, only one cure for the depression and humiliation such cold approaches created - a good stiff drink. I just couldn't leave it.

Seemingly, the only persons who didn't turn their backs on me were my wife Margaret and my mother. Mother welcomed me back to my typewriter with two or three little temperance lectures.

I can remember her standing with the open Bible in her hand and saying, "It's not the end of the world yet for you son. In God's Name try and rid yourself of that cursed stuff for all time and keep writing. People continually tell me how much they enjoy your pieces in the paper. And son, think of your lovely wife and family. Give your boys and girls a bright and decent future. You can do it with your writing and music ... please, please son, try your best."

But in a couple of hours time, mother's earnest pleas were being washed from my thoughts by the liquid she hated so much and which had given her a life-long span of torture.

I had been too quick in condemning Daisy as a weak fool and senseless chicken, for that glass of cheap wine I had taken at the Irish Wake so many years ago had completed its course of destruction. I now craved drink every minute of the day. It had now become my god and master!

In a short time I had finished working in my mother's home. I shook so much in the mornings that I couldn't handle the typewriter until, of course, I had those steadying drinks. I was now scribbling my articles by pen in the corner of a pub and slipping them into the editorial office. My employers were very tolerant towards my absenteeism with the hope that I sobered and returned to being useful.

But that didn't seem possible, for I was going down and down with funds now inadequate to sustain my thirst. So desperate was I for money that I had sold my saxophone and fishing gear. Then the sad afternoon came that I was forced to go to my mother's home for the typewriter. The old woman was greatly saddened that I had not only left her, but no longer visited her.

As I carried the typewriter out of her home I could see the agony on her wrinkled face. Was she dreading the possibility of losing a son to the curse of her life as well as a husband? But my only concern was getting a few pounds for the article in my hands.

I had another degrading way of getting drink. I would take my banjo into pubs and play selections and when the drinks doubled up I had an empty bottle at my feet which I soon filled and took home with me. If I didn't have it when in bed horrible frightening illusions floated in front of my eyes. As well as being my master the content of the bottle was my protector.

Chapter
FIFTEEN

ALCOHOL ADDICTION HAD ALSO MADE ME A SELF-CENTRED SCHEMING AND LYING SLAVE TO ITS indescribable craving. Local banks, wine marts, pubs and even business houses, had my name in heavy red print in their debt books. They no longer were providing the vital morning cure and steadier for head and shakes. And changing circumstances had downgraded the medicine to a ten-glass bottle of wine costing five shillings and eleven pence and better known to decent society as 'gutrot.'

My wardrobe had somehow emptied itself and the only clothes I had to cover me was a threadbare two-piece suit, in need of a clean and press and the shoes on my feet were beyond a cobbler's power to repair.

I wasn't writing newspaper articles any more nor playing music, for even the old banjo had gone for a song. And indeed, any wee bit of culture and the magnet for inspiration that were within me had also disappeared.

Only the chronic alcoholic knows the agony of the appalling morning sickness he brings upon himself - a head like concrete, terrible dizziness and shaking and sweating. Yet, stranger than fiction, the dope that causes those uncontrollable tortures is the cure for them.

While shaking I had to get help to enable me to swallow the first and second drinks out of glass or bottle. Then the swallowing went on normally, probably without food, until my eyes closed in a drunken doze. This may seem ludicrous, but, believe me, it is only too true.

One morning I was in distress for my morning steadying medicine. I hadn't any money and there were no signs of any coming and my shakes were getting worse. As I sat on a seat at Coleraine Diamond, I had my hands in my trouser pockets trying to hide them and at the same time steady them.

Then across my troubled mind appeared a vision of my mother. I hadn't visited her since collecting the typewriter and that was months past. But maybe I could bear one of her strict temperance lectures this morning and afterwards try and borrow some money from her. She had drawn her old-age pension yesterday.

I strolled up to Long Commons and knocking on 79 my mother opened the door in quick response. She looked greyer and even more wrinkled on the brow and her greeting was rather abrupt.

"It's near about time you came to see your old mother." she said. "I haven't been hearing good reports about you and its very worrying."

"Aye, there's always some one with tales to tell." I retorted. "They just can't mind their own business."

Mother studied me up and down and her tone was softer as she replied: "You can't deny that you're not very sick, son. Look at you shake all over." Then rising she suggested a fry of bacon and egg.

I lied that I just had a meal, so she made me toast and a mug of tea and she couldn't have made me anything more embarrassing, for my efforts to lift either were utterly hopeless.

Mother, weeping sorely, pulled her chair close to mine at the table and then holding my head began feeding me. "It's just like I used to do at Abbey Street," she sobbed, "but you were innocent. clean and healthy then. Oh how time changes things ... sadly, in my case, for the worse."

Feeding time over I started talking. "Mammy," I lied again, "I'm here to tell you that I'm giving the drink up from today and I'll soon be back at my writing and music."

"That is the moment I've prayed for." mother exclaimed, placing her right hand on the ever open Bible as a token of confidence.

"I've a few preparations to make mammy," I said trying to sound appealing, "I was wondering if you've a pound you can lend me? I'll let you have it back soon?"

Mother obliged and I left her standing at the door. She was still there when I turned the corner into Newmarket Street, the woman I had deceived yet again - the woman who bore me, slaved for me and loved me. I reflected on her right hand on the open Bible and for the first time ever my self-centred attitude softened. Sentiment had somehow sparked off in the background to challenge the power of alcohol. Was there anything happening?

FAREWELL

Mother's loan certainly got me rid of the shakes that horrible morning and later I was to meet my wife Margaret downtown. Amazingly, she had stood by me during my degrading spans of turmoil and had her big share of pain and humiliation. Yes, to such a degree beyond description.

In a matter of hours I had experienced my second pang of emotion and it was then I was suddenly possessed of the desire for sobriety and walked home with my heroine telling her of my determination to try pulling myself together for her and the family's sake, my mother's sake and my own.

I did manage to abstain from drinking for a few agonising days, in the course of which, sister Annie sought me and said: "Mother has had a wee turn and I would like you to give me a hand upstairs with her ... she's not able any more to climb them."

Going to number 79 my mother was no longer in receiving mood with those gesturing hands and non-stop tongue. Instead, she sat starring at the kitchen ceiling in silence, a stance that was not becoming to her. Oh no! No! No!

We carried the frail figure of mother upstairs and after Annie had put her to bed I returned to the room and felt sad as I pulled a chair up to the bedside. Silence still prevailed and it was awful! If only mother would speak she could scold me, lecture to me on temperance or even preach a full sermon out of the Book she knew so well, and I would listen.

But an hour later, the old woman was able to communicate a little to prove that her mental faculties were intact and that was uplifting. The fact, however, that degeneration had set in and taken away her strength, couldn't be hidden.

As I sat there by that sick bedside not knowing what to say or do I actually wished, if a bit audaciously, that I had been a better son. It came to me that I had failed mother hopelessly in return for the multitude of sacrifices she had made for me. Yet, I've got to state again, the only favour she ever asked of me was that I grew up to be decent and sober.

Even as my Lady of Long Commons lay there with death looming closely above, her eyes never left me ... gentle eyes still proclaiming her love for me.

And what was the wayward son's response to this heart-rending scene? Continuing temperance? Sadly, no. I accepted it as an excuse to drown my sorrows and soon was back in the straits of despair. I was an utter impossibility!

Mary Edith Moore, age 88, died on May, 23rd, 1959. Her burial in Coleraine cemetery evoked rivers of tears from all who knew her goodness, humility and love. As I stood there at the grave side weeping and shaking I had yet another desire for sobriety.

RECOVERED

In 1961, a regular attender of Alcoholic Anonymous, I had recovered from my drink problem and was back writing for the Chronicle. We had further broadened our horizons to gain the prestigious title 'Ulster's Premier Provincial Weekly'.

I had established a page 'People & Places' and was really enjoying writing it. I didn't seem to have lost any of the flair for spotlighting people and featuring them and so I went on and on progressing and was also back playing the banjo and saxophone more lively and brighter than ever. And, principally, things at home were prosperous and happy.

To add to this all round success and good behaviour I had a book 'Smiles and Tears' published in 1972. The launching of the book took place in a Portstewart Hotel and it was there tragedy struck at me through my own downright foolishness. I was tempted to have one drink at the toast of success and that was followed by an unending binge which again stripped me of my possessions and put me at the bottom end of 'Skid Row,' the drunkards term for the lowest ebb of humanity.

I should explain that Margaret and I had six bonnie children - Nina, Edith, Willis, Christine, Valerie and Adrian. Nina, married name, Nina McAuley, had eight equally bonnie children - Sharon, Deborah, Moore, Derek, Nicola, Janice, Gary and Jill.

Nina was the bright shining star and counsellor of our family circle. When a member had a spot of trouble of any kind he or she went along to the one they loved and trusted and aways came away enlightened.

We became greatly perturbed when the hardworking and seemingly healthy Nina had a mysterious ailment in her right foot, which spread to both legs and cruelly paralysed her. The result was confinement to a wheelchair.

Showing tremendous courage, Nina entered hospitals in Belfast and London and underwent operation after operation by leading surgeons in a bid to walk. Doctors, nurses, domestic staff and fellow sufferers, acclaimed her the perfect patient and the life soul of the ward. Her personality and sense of humour were very special and made her company keenly sought.

But behind Nina's never fading smile and non-complaining attitude was a deep concern for my drink problem and she often let me know about it and rendered sound advice, which, sadly, I didn't accept.

It was at this time an extraordinary incident occurred. Once a month Nina attended a Divine Healing Ministry in First Coleraine Presbyterian Church, which was conducted by the Revd Dr James McFarland. She was mostly taken there by her husband Victor, but one morning he was unavailable and as a last resort I was asked to oblige.

I agreed wholeheartedly, but was worried about carrying Nina up the steep step of the church to her wheelchair, for I had little strength due to the lack of food. Booze was my sole sustenance.

And that physical weakness was to be the cause of my failure in the errand of mercy. I just managed to carry Nina on to the upper step and was placing her in the wheelchair when my back gave a loud crack! I dropped to the ground in agonising pain whining like a wounded hare and thinking that I had fractured my spine.

The Revd James Kane, a ministry steward, helped me to my feet and led me into the church, where I became a priority figure for the healing chair at the request of Nina and the other disabled folk.

Soon I was ushered into the chair and then Dr McFarland laid hands on me and prayed for my recovery. But I had neither faith nor belief in what was said. Two things occupied my fuddled mind - the danger of permanent injury and a certain pub two streets away.

Eventually I arrived at the pub with my tale of woe. I was agonisingly stooped, a position I had to adapt to give me some little ease. And in spite of having tried doctors and rub specialists this terrible new malady persisted, which was not pleasant on top of my problem.

MENTAL AND PHYSICAL WRECK

On a March morning in 1976 while wandering around a mental and physical wreck, I had two thoughts in mind. One was the River Bann and the other a doctor named Bill Holley who, as a devout Christian, evinced a keen interest in alcoholics.

Fortunately, I got past the river and arrived at the doctor's surgery. He received me and then studying my dishevelled form calculatingly, said: "You're in poor shape."

"Yes, doctor," I explained, "I'm completely beat by the shakes and sweats and horrible notions of suicide."

The doctor looked me up and down again in a pondering sort of way and said: "Instead of sending you to Gransha, would you go to Hopefield Hospital, Portrush, if I got you admitted there?"

"I'll go anywhere you suggest doctor." I replied.

The kindly doctor made arrangements on the phone and so the following afternoon, a very nervous and shaking character, I entered Hopefield Hospital and was welcomed by a highly efficient, understanding and charming member of nursing staff, then Sister Maura O'Kane, who directed me to the isolation ward and after fitting me out with pyjamas and dressing gown, gave me a tablet to calm the shakes and keep me from exploding in the absence of the alcohol.

The ward was quite comfortable with a big window looking out on a pleasant country scene. But there was one thing I wasn't too fussy about - a New Testament sat on the locker beside the bed. Why couldn't I have a bunch of randy magazines to suit my way of living, but definitely not 'this book.' It would remain unopened.

Seven days later and still in bitter agnostic mood, I pulled the dressing gown over the pyjamas and went shuffling round the hospital on my weak legs, just for something to do, for I was desperately lonely and depressed, fully realising that I was at the end of my tether.

Going into a big main ward my attention was drawn to an old white-haired male patient sitting at a small table at the side of his bed and he was reading a large book through a magnifying glass.

Next day when in the same ward I noticed that the patient was still reading the large book. Curiosity gripped me and so I slipped across the ward and peeped over the old man's shoulder to discover that the book he was showing so much interest in was the Holy Bible.

Then a nurse passed on the information that the patient was the Revd John Beatie, a former Church of Ireland rector and he had reached the ripe old age of 92.

I couldn't get the hang of this. A clergyman of 92, who should have had the contents of the Bible digested ten times over, yet there he was still reading at it intensely.

The situation was certainly puzzling, especially to an agnostic like myself. What was there in that tattered old book that this man could not separate himself from? What was the magnetic power that commanded his dedication morning and afternoon?

REDEEMED

On one occasion I was compelled to interrupt his reverence's reading and put this question to him: "What do you get out of reading that book continually?"

Leaving the magnifying glass on the table the old man looked up, smiled benignly and replied: "My dear boy, every time I look at this book I'm the recipient of something beautifully new and inspiring, which instils in me solace and hope. This book is the rock of mankind and each of us should have a sound footing on it, so that we may find the pathway to lasting life with the Holy Father."

Speechless, I shuffled back to the isolation ward and after sitting on the bed pondering over the old clergyman's words, I lifted the New Testament from the locker and browsed over it. On the inside front page I noticed the name Gideons and that they were the suppliers of the literature. I wondered who the Gideons were.

Then closing and leaving the testament back on the locker I wandered back to the Reverend John's ward. I was finding there an escape from the frightening reflections that continually haunted my moments alone.

And I was to further discover that my new companion was a delightful conversationalist and a remarkable raconteur. He would speak about dear old Donegal with inordinate pride. "My parish there was one of poor land and many stones, but every single member of my flock had a heart of gold and my meagre stipend was greatly enlarged by the sincerity of their friendship and simple faith."

He also spoke of Pettigoe, his parish in County Fermanagh, in affectionate terms and with traces of nostalgia. "Oh how well my parishioners there treated me. And I still have a lot of thought for them when the lights go out at night, a splendid time to reminisce and extol the lovely things that have happened in years gone by."

And though he didn't push religion down one's throat, he never concealed the fact of his strong Christian beliefs. At the end of one of our chats he said: "At my age, dear friend, the flesh is a heavy burden to carry, but I'm consoled by the scriptural information that this world is not our home, so patiently I await the Master's call."

Back in the isolation ward I could only sit and think and think. I was amazed at the Reverend John's impeccable faith. There he was waiting to die with joy in his heart, knowing that after his last breath he was going somewhere special to begin a lasting life and here I was, a confounded drunk, continually possessed of suicidal tendencies, but never had the guts to take my own life because of the fear and uncertainty of the beyond. I was in a big black pit of despair - hopelessly lost!

Somehow not pitying myself, as usual, I got into bed still thinking deeply on the Reverend John's words: "The Bible is the rock of mankind."

Next morning when I awoke something very strange happened. I lifted the Gideon New Testament with my shaking hands and opening it at random my eyes fell upon verse nine of Luke eleven and this warm invitation. "And I say unto you, ask and it shall be given you, seek and ye shall find, knock, and the door shall be opened unto you."

As the wee bits of religion I had learned at my mother's knee came back to me vividly I wept as I could see in my mind's eye that lovely man Jesus hanging on that crude wood structure, bleeding from that mock crown of thorns, horse whipped and dying for a drunken rascal like me.

I crawled out of bed and shuffled over to the window. It was a nice April morning in 1976 with the countryside beginning to wear its spring dress and I felt that God was speaking to me through this. He wanted to help me in my terrible plight.

Closing my eyes I prayed as best as I knew how and a glow of joy overwhelmed me as I was gloriously redeemed.

Chapter
SIXTEEN

MY CONVERSION AND DIVINE HEALING, NATURALLY,
REMAINS WITH ME AS THE MOST SENSATIONAL
happening of my entire life. One minute I was a deep-in-sin
agnostic and in the next a born-again Christian. Let me briefly
describe my reaction to the sudden transformation.

The gnawing pain in my back and the shakes and sweats
symptoms had gone and I was possessed of a feeling of confidence.
When breakfast was served I ate every crumb of it, something I
couldn't attempt before. And on the nurse arriving with the once
vital and much craved tablet, I smiled and told her I didn't need it as
a lovely man named Jesus had put a healing hand upon me. Scared
looking the nice wee lass hastened from the ward thinking, I'm sure,
that he has gone stark mad!

I was a complete new creature, gloriously happy and the
depressing thoughts of what the future held and the mountains of
debts I had to face on my discharge from hospital, which had been

plaguing me the last few days, had become a mere challenge to my new-found strength.

I phoned my daughter Nina at her home and told her that something wonderful had happened to me and that I had finished with drink for all time.

Her reply was: "Great news daddy! Now I'm going to ask you to go back to the morning you sat in the healing chair in First Coleraine Presbyterian Church. You really had little respect for Doctor McFarland's sincere prayer. But I'm going to tell you daddy that was the moment God began to take an interest in you."

And it was nice that my exemplary sister Annie should hear of my salvation before her death. Her rejoicing was great!

That very special conversion Sunday, I spent reading the New Testament in my ward, knowing that the Revd John liked Sundays all to himself. But after another hearty breakfast on Monday morning I carried the glad tidings to his ward.

"Wonderful! Wonderful!" he exclaimed, clapping his withered hands, "It looks like we're going to meet one day on that Heavenly Shore after all."

A short time later the devoted Christian was called to his Eternal Reward. His funeral procession to Ballywillan Cemetery consisted of four mourners. But oh how I would have loved to have witnessed his arrival in Gloryland! I'm sure that was some reception with the greeting: "Well done, true and faithful servant."

I was soon to discover, however, that all clergymen didn't have the witnessing qualities of the Revd John Beatie, nor the gift of making people like myself feel equal to him and very much at ease in his company.

One afternoon as I lay in bed in the isolation ward, my eyes glued to the Gideon New Testament, the door got a knock and then opened wide to show the figure of a gentlemen of the cloth.

"May I come in?" he asked.

"Of course." I replied, thinking gleefully that I was going to get a religious talk and prayer to further strengthen my wonderful joyous feeling.

But to my surprise the visitor withdrew a packet of cigarettes from his pocket and bringing one out, lit it and sat on a chair at the side of my bed puffing, obviously more interested in the satisfaction of his much condemned worldly habit than in a golden opportunity to proclaim the gospel message to one just beginning his Christian walk with its obstacles.

Half-way through his cigarette the clergyman spoke. "It's my day for visiting patients here" he explained, "and it's nice to get a minute or two of relaxation and a deserving smoke to sooth and refresh one."

I gave instant thought to his remark and my own situation and felt hurt. What was I other than a patient that there were no words of comfort or prayer conveyed? Was I just a 'nobody' occupying the isolation ward - a place for a smoke?

He left hurriedly without as much as a parting 'Goodbye' or 'So long.' But Dr Holley that evening informed me that I would meet with such abrupt incidents. I had to realise that personal prayer was the answer and belief in God's precious promise that He would never leave me.

Somewhat prepared for the big task ahead I went home and while many people rejoiced at my conversion there were those who mocked and laughed at it. The betting in the pubs was heavy. 'Three to one Speedy will be back on the bottle before Saturday.' 'Four to one he'll back in a fortnight.' 'Seven to one he and the old banjo will be back with us in a month.' 'He just couldn't stay away ... pubs are his life!'

But the gamblers had grossly underestimated the power of Almighty God - the God who can do anything but fail. When He touched Speedy that victorious Sunday morning, He made a good sound job of him, not only spiritually, but mentally and physically.

GIDEONS

I was keen to find out who the Gideons were and eventually did secure the information. The world-wide movement comprise business and professional men who subscribe to the printing of tens of thousands of Bibles and New Testaments which are given free to the pupils of schools (Catholic and Protestant), hotels, prisons and hospitals, with the belief that its message will be an answer to the problems and pressures of the critical days in which we live.

Let me deal with one subject I know all about. Trauma and tragedy frequently result in time spent in hospital. Admission more often than not produces anxiety and fear. At such times patients look for reassurance, comfort and encouragement. The Gideons have found that the true source of such help is found in Jesus, Who reveals Himself in the Bible. I can definately endorse that sentiment from my personal experience.

One of the things I had concern for was how I was going to mix with certain Christian folk I had often miscalled for adhering to their faith and I would have crossed to the other side of the street to avoid meeting them face to face.

But one of them put me at ease one day with the news that they were praying for me all the time. Praying for an obnoxious character who hated them? Astonishing!

My debts disappeared one after the other and I had managed to climb my way back into decent society. In addition to those virtues, Margaret and I had got a wee new home away from the bitter memories of the old one and life was gloriously happy. It truly was a home worthy of the name.

And I had not only resumed my 'People & Places' feature in the Chronicle, but had started a Church Page, which was serving all denominations and doing well.

NERVOUS EXPERIENCE

My position in town had become a rare one. People, some of whom were known to me and some who were not, would stop me on the street and kiss and hug me and welcome me into God's family circle of which they implied they were staunch members. Then the invitations pored out of them. "You'll have to join us in our home for fellowship and tea ... we'll get in touch."

The majority of those invitations proved to be negative. The novelty of the drunk's conversion had caused quite a sensation in town and they wanted to get in on the act. But when the novelty subsided a bit those same people passed me by without notice. Their meaningless 'hot air' did not impress me and issued a clear warning that even in Christian ranks there were 'enthusiasts' whose word I had to be careful about accepting.

I had been nine months strictly on the water-wagon, yet I can't say that I hadn't thought of a drink. I often did, especially after a day's fishing on the River Roe. But this time I had the strength and common sense to fight and defeat any cravings. That powerful spirit within my soul carried me through.

However, I've got to confess I was only a lukewarm Christian sticking to the faith simply because it was keeping me sober. I had done nothing for God in reciprocation for His merciful deliverance, except my simple prayers of thanks.

But Dr T.B.F. Thompson was soon to change that lackadaisical routine. I had gone to a Rev. Sammy Workman Mission, in the C.W.U. Hall, Garvagh, with which T.B.F. is closely associated, to photograph a Ballymena Musical Group for the Chronicle Church Page.

When I was about to leave the hall, T.B.F. asked me if I would return to the mission one evening and give a word of testimony, to which I shook my head incessantly.

But the gentleman persisted and so in the end I agreed and there and then a date was arranged.

In the days that followed I was very nervous about the complications that could set in during my assignment. There's bound to be a crowd of fellows present I used to booze with and they would be ribbing me from all angles. Of course, they would be accepting my appearance in a Christian pulpit as a big joke!

I was so petrified that I sat down to write to T.B.F. and cancel the whole affair, but somehow I couldn't. And so on the evening I was to testify my wife Margaret and I drove to Garvagh with me praying fervently all the way. Entering the town we found cars parked on each side of the Coleraine Road.

"There must be something big on in town tonight?" I said.

"Probably a dance in the Imperial hotel." came the reply,

But it was no dance the cars had come for. They had brought people to hear the ex-drunk from Coleraine tell his story. And I continued to pray: "Dear God, please , please, stay with me this evening."

The hall was packed to capacity. I even had to squeeze my way into the pulpit, it also being occupied by people, apart from the preacher.

I spoke for twenty minutes and contrary to my expectations that there would be interruptions, everything went well. Indeed, as the old saying goes. "One could have heard a pin drop!" Yes, I must say it again that the liberty I had on that momentous occasion was quite amazing.

A couple of days later a Presbyterian clergyman approached me and asked if I would testify for him at one of his Sunday evening after-church meetings in the Church Hall. It was a new venture and not a very successful one with only some twenty people turning up at a hall capable of seating four hundred comfortably.

I agreed to attend and the clergyman advertised in the local press that I was to appear and it certainly paid big dividends, for the hall was full on the Sunday evening of the meeting. Many of the folk, I would say, were there to satisfy their curiosities.

All smiles the clergyman shook my hand briskly to honour the success of the event then he invited me into a small room where he immediately put the question to me. "How long does this testimony you've prepared for this evening last?"

"I was twenty minutes in the pulpit at Garvagh, but having improved it I may be twenty-five minutes this evening."

The clergyman stroked his chin and then looking at me said demandingly: "I would like you to cut the testimony to a minimum ... say five or six minutes, for after my message I've got to hurry and give the epilogue at a Youth Rally in Limavady."

I was shocked! Never in my life could I remember being more humiliated by a fellow human's words. Possessed of a temperamental nature I thought about charging out of the hall, but that force within me quelled my haste and so I went into the pulpit paying no attention to what the clergyman wanted and I was provided with yet another marvellous twenty minutes of liberty ... and it could have been twenty five or thirty minutes. I never bothered looking at my watch.

On an unforgettable Sunday morning in January, 1987, my dear daughter Nina passed on and I never realised until then that it was possible to experience the sense of poignancy that welled up in me. I was speechless for hours. The tears just wouldn't stop.

But I was to find some consolation in the words of Revd David McIlwrath, who conducted the service prior to interment. He said:

"The only thing that will survive death is Christian character. Our citizenship is in Heaven and God's future purposes are a new body."

EXCITING ENGAGEMENT

Dr Thompson had certainly started something moving when he put me in the C.W.U. pulpit in Garvagh that unforgettable night, for later I was to testify in every corner of Britain, including Shetland, Orkney, the western Isles, the Isle of Man, the Irish Republic and Canada, where I televised not only to that country, but the United States. The programme was named 'One Hundred Huntley Street.' I also appeared on British National and Northern Ireland television and broadcast from many radio stations.

I trust this does not sound boastful in any way. Such was widely revealed to glorify God's Name and give proof of His mercy, love and willingness to transform a helpless wreck and then use him as a witness for His Kingdom. Thankfully, it is known that quite a number of alcoholics found peace through the medium of my testimony. May many more come forward.

As I sit meditating I'm prompted to include one of my most exciting engagements. After dinner on a very special evening I was to speak at the Annual Convention of British Gideons International in the Metropole Hotel, Birmingham.

I was staying overnight in the hotel and my room number was 1072, yet I was only half-way along the second floor. I think it was six floors I saw on the lift sign, so you can guess the vast dimensions of the building and realise that it was little wonder an Irish country lad got lost three times before finding the auditorium, in which hundreds and hundreds of people sat.

Soon I was called in front of those people from all parts of the British Isles and as the mass of faces faded into the distance I suddenly went back to Hopefield Hospital's isolation ward, where I could see myself sitting with the New Testament in my hand wondering who the Gideons were who had supplied the book. Now here I was about to commend their widespread ministry and tell them the story of the powerful impact it had on my sinful existence. The liberty I received was stupendous.

Before flying out of Birmingham the next day I had a long list of new-found friends which I still try to keep in touch with. Their kindness and warmth made me feel that it was just great being a Christian, absolutely free from the cravings of alcohol, nicotine and gambling.

Back home again a couple of nice things happened to me which I wish to mention with gratitude. Ron Finlay, boss of Finlay Textiles, Londonderry, Coleraine and Portstewart, presented me with an expensive G banjo to add some music to my little ministry.

And one Saturday afternoon when I was covering the Coleraine Agricultural Show for the press, a Tannoy message called me to the President's Office, where a note lay on the table. It was from Mae and Willie Whyte, then owners of the Whitehaven Furniture Company, Portstewart, and it read. "You have played the saxophone a long time for the devil, now start playing one for the Lord. Go to Johnnie Owens Music Shop, Ballymoney, and take your pick of instruments."

What a wonderful gesture. A brand new Selmer Alto Saxophone. I got to learning popular hymns on the instrument and always found willing organists and pianists to accompany me and so Mae and Willie Whyte's favourite piece 'How Great Thou Art' became my signature number and justifiably I feel.

I was to record a saxophone cassette, appropriately named 'He Touched Me' and it was commended in a letter from a fellow saxophonist in the U.S.A., the President, himself, Bill Clinton.

VICTOR HUTCHINSON

Victor Hutchinson requires no introduction from me. He is known in numerous homes throughout the British Isles and the Republic of Ireland, which are brightened and blessed by his gospel records, cassettes and videos. This international service, involving massive sales, has rewarded him with both gold and silver discs.

A top singer with a hearty and rousing style, a delightful accordionist and a preacher of tremendous ability, Victor took me under his wing and we found to our pleasing that my saxophone and banjo blended perfectly with his giant electronic accordion and soon our ministry was in demand, not only in Ireland, but across the Channel in England, Scotland and Wales.

Our very first tour of Scotland comes to mind with pleasant memories. Victor had hired a motor van and the first meeting in Stranraer was a huge success, which opened the way for a four day tour of Galloway.

Comprising Wigtownshire, Kirkcudbright and the southern part of Ayrshire, the very name Galloway has a lilt to it and within its boundaries there exists a variety of countryside that suits, so to speak, every mood. Landward, there are scenes as emerald green as Ireland's north west and, seaward, there are lovely golden beaches seemingly everywhere. And it is richly endowed with hills and glens and lochs and rivers that thrilled my angling heart.

In Scotland, Victor and I felt very much at home, for we both claim to be Ulster Scots and the people we met there certainly treated us like blood brothers. That tour proved to be so wonderful that we were encouraged to return again and again until we had covered the whole of the country.

FLYING MINISTRY

Victor and I had invitations to conduct Praise Rallies in distant places such as Shetland, Orkney, and the Inner and Outer Hebrides. Victor, a chief government social worker and I just could not afford the time it would have taken to get to those places by road and sea.

But eventually my energetic friend found a way. Approaching me one day he said: "Do you like flying?"

"No, it makes my arms ache." I quipped in return.

Laughing he explained that he had got an aircraft and an experienced pilot to take us and the equipment to the out of the way places.

I gave the matter some thought and in the end agreed and soon had fifteen hours flying experience in my logbook. Victor did better, for he became hooked on the art of flying, and after extensive training qualified as a pilot.

We were now flying to all venue's across Channel and I was made to feel more at ease with two pilots in the small single engine plane. But not so on the day we were coming in to land at Glasgow Airport. Victor, then in his flying infancy, was in charge of controls and Michael made no effort to take them. Sportingly he wanted his friend to gain confidence.

As the wheels touched the runway my head almost went through the roof of the plane and when things had calmed a bit and we were on our way to the traffic control area I leaned forward and said to Michael, "What was that landing of Victor's like?"

"Which one?" he asked.

A GREAT AND DARING AVIATOR

Michael Kirk had a delightful sense of humour and was not only a charming fellow in every way, but   a great and daring pilot. How could I forget the day we left Aghadowey's old wartime airfield for a Praise Rally in the Scottish Island of Westray, situated 25 miles from Orkney,

I had full confidence in Michael getting us to our destination as usual. However, that confidence sagged when Highlands Traffic Control announced that all flying was banned in the Westray area due to treacherous gales.

Michael looked at Victor and said determinedly: "We have a Rally to fulfil this evening, so we're going on in spite of the warning."

The small plane, being battered by ugly blasts which put it in all shapes, somehow kept moving forward, the engine at full throttle. As I cowed in the seat with my head hid in a coat, it seemed my stomach was coming up through the back of my neck. And I was praying aloud.

Then I heard Michael shouting into the phone to someone on the island, instructing him to have four strong men, two at each side, to grab the wings of the plane, if he managed to land.

The pilot made the grass runway safely and the four men got hold of the plane's wings until it was tethered, not only to our own relief, but to the relief of those islanders who had watched the sky epic with prayers on their lips.

On removing myself from the back seat, thanking God that I was still in one piece, I felt like kissing the ground but reneged when I was pushed into a ring to receive a hero's welcome with Michael and Victor. It was then my shrunk chest began to expand a bit.

I was to fly with Michael and Victor on many flights until the sad day Michael was killed when his plane crashed near to his Ballymena farm. Victor and I officiated at the funeral and our farewell to a dear and true friend was endorsed by hundreds of mourners.

In my old age I feel just great having the security of a place in that Mansion in the sky where I'm going to have a reunion with all of my dear ones and hear mother's words. "You made it in the end son."